The Story of
Northumberland Park
North Shields
Spital Dene and The Pow Burn

Mike N. Coates

Dedicated to
Wilfred George Coates
8th July 1911 to 9th February 2012

Who still with an inquiring mind at the age of 100
was an inspiration to all who knew him.

Previous page: This picture is a postcard posted in December 1907 of the main park entrance on King Edward Road and was taken by J W Sawyer of Tynemouth Road, North Shields a local commercial photographer. The identity of the gentleman in the carriage is unknown.

Copyright Mike N. Coates 2012
First published in 2012
ISBN: 978-1-906721-52-7

Published by Summerhill Books, Newcastle-upon-Tyne
www.summerhillbooks.co.uk
email: summerhillbooks@yahoo.co.uk

Contents

Introduction

My interest in Northumberland Park arose from the fact that I lived in Park Avenue overlooking the Bowling Greens from the age of four till twenty two and spent the majority of my childhood when "playing out" in Northumberland Park. My paternal grandfather had lived in Park Avenue forty years previously and I played bowls in my teenage years with my maternal grandfather who was a member of Northumberland Bowling Club. My earliest memories are of the gardeners pushing me around in their wheelbarrows as the park at that time with a staff of 9 gardeners and 2 Park keepers was a safe and adventurous playground for pre-computer age children who spent all available playing time out of doors.

As children growing up in the 1950's and 60's (before daytime television and computers which now keep children indoors for their recreation) we met our friends and amused ourselves mainly on the playing field swings and roundabouts. On the Tea-pot Lid which by running around in the centre whilst pushing against the centre bars, you could create a centrifugal force if not to throw any passengers off at least make them scream for mercy or as a passenger to attempt to hang on as long as possible to the outside bars whilst your legs would seem to attempt to drag you into orbit. The Witches Hat or Ocean Wave as we preferred to call it on which you could hang onto the outside seats and run as fast as possible, regularly losing contact with the ground as it rose and fell or by pulling around in the centre, cause it to sway in and out while rotating giving the fainter hearted seasickness without leaving dry land. In the interests of that 'spoilsport' Health and Safety, first the Banana Slide had a safety cage erected on the top in 1957, stopping us climbing up the supporting poles and clambering onto the top instead of using the steps and then in 1961 the Tea-pot Lid and Ocean Wave were removed altogether. We built dens, climbed every tree possible, made rope swings on trees on the steepest slopes, played marbles and conkers and roller skated (bikes forbidden) and knew every bush and hiding place, even holding competitions to see who could run the quickest bent double, carrying a torch through the pitch darkness of the culvet at the top of the pond to the golf course and back.

My observations of the changing seasons and the arrival and departure of migrating birds developed my interest in ornithology. Then along with data collated from trapping birds using Mist Nets supplied by The British Trust for Ornithology to study population changes and migration in 1974, I produced a booklet entitled "The Birds of Northumberland Park" – a copy of which is in North Shields Library.

After 30 years I thought it was time to update this booklet but since I had meanwhile researched the history of St Leonard's Hospital and the Dene area in general I decided to collate all the information I could regarding the history as well as the natural history of the area and present it in the form of this book.

Mike N. Coates, 2012

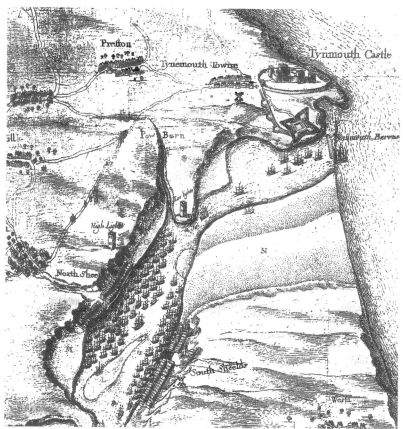

NORTH SHIELDS and POW BURN in 1655.

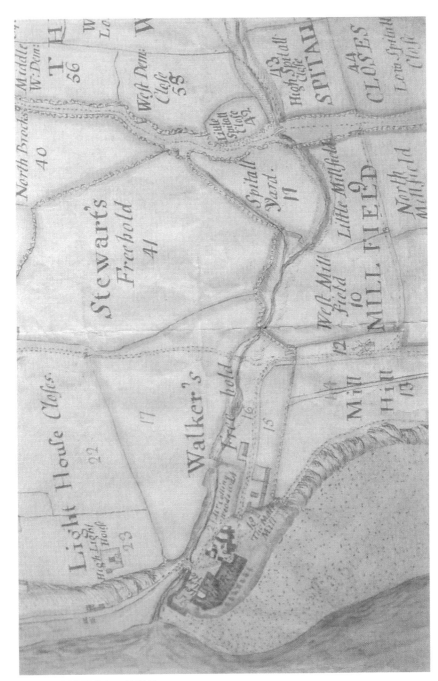

POW BURN in 1757.

SPITAL DENE in 1865.

NORTHUMBERLAND PARK IN 1896.

SPITAL DENE in 1935.

Historical Notes on the Pow Burn and Spital Dene

The Pow Burn probably derived its name from the Celtic name for a stream "pwl" and from old maps it appears to have originated in an area known as "The Mosses" which lay between the present Marden and Preston Grange Estates and entered the north bank of the River Tyne where the Fish Quay is now situated.

North Shields owes its existence to the humble Pow Burn for in 1225, Prior Germanus of Tynemouth Priory and his monks reclaimed a large area of marshy ground by the burn by draining it and gave permission for 7 sheels/shiels (small thatched huts) to be built, each with their own quay, between the Pow Burn and the sikket (ditch) to the west. In return for this favour they were to provide fish for the monastery.

The mouth of the Pow Burn was the first safe harbour on the north side of the River Tyne and it was not long before merchants and traders realised the benefit of this landing place so near to the mouth of the Tyne. By 1292 there was in excess of a hundred houses here, many of which had their own quays; the principal trades being brewing and baking. Trade increased to such an extent that the Burgesses of Newcastle, jealous of their loss of trade further up the river, gained the support of Edward I. A trial was held in 1306, judgement was given in parliament and the Prior of Tynemouth was fined five marks and had to dismantle the jetties at his own cost. The town, now known as North Shields (to differentiate it from the township of South Shields on the opposite bank of the Tyne) was forbidden to hold a fair or market and vessels were forbidden to load or unload at Shields. The King objected because part of Newcastle's revenue belonged to him whereas North Shields revenue belonged entirely to the Priors.

This dispute over Newcastle's monopoly of river trade lasted for hundreds of years and in 1652 Ralph Gardner of Chirton was imprisoned for refusing to close his brewery in North Shields. In 1655 from his prison cell he petitioned Oliver Cromwell's Parliament in a document entitled "England's Grievance" for an abolition of Newcastle's restrictions upon trade and although his petition was unsuccessful in the mid 17th century an act was passed to re-establish the quays and market and from that time the town again prospered.

A memorial to Ralph Gardner, was erected in 1882, opposite to the site where his cottage once stood.

Products were loaded from a quay at the west side of the Pow Burn the remains of which, in the form of a frame of oak beams and hollowed out tree trunks used for conveying water were discovered about twelve feet below the surface by workmen excavating for a gasometer at the bottom of Brewhouse Bank in September 1819.

On Fryer's map of 1772-3 a group of buildings is shown as a **Brewery** which had water brought from reservoirs at Percy Main and Whitley in wooden pipes to ensure a good supply. This brewery was owned by John Walker and in 1797 was let to Henry Coward of New Whitley. Coward was also let an area of ground called the "Salt Marsh" on the east side of the Pow Burn, bounded by what is now Union Street/Tanners Bank. By 1857 the brewery was known as the Low Lights Brewery. The land still belonged to the Walker family.

Evans plan of 1803 shows a long north-south range of buildings labelled "Mr Walker's Brewhouse". Carr Ormeston and Carr were described in 1876-7 (Christie) as brewers at Brewery Bank and maltsters at Low Lights.

The Old Maltings was part of their complex and the Low Lights Brewery of Carr Brothers was amalgamated with Newcastle Breweries when it became a limited company in 1890.

The Old Maltings which is a late 18th/ early 19th century sandstone building with Welsh slate roof was later used as a smoke house and has more recently been converted for use as workshops by the North Shields Grinding Company.

11

In 1765 a Quaker, John Richardson, the son of William who manufactured leather in his tannery at Great Ayton and Whitby moved to a farm at Seghill East New Houses where he struggled for 6 years but couldn't make a decent living. So he returned to the family trade and with his wife and three children, took a piece of ground and a small farm called "Pew Dene" which was near the Low Lights Lighthouse, then a popular bathing place. He pastured his horse and cattle on the high banks and built his house and established a **Tannery** in 1766 on the low ground by the side of the Pow Burn. It developed into a large and lucrative business, tanning hides, calfskins and sealskins which were brought into the port by whalers and operated until 1890 when the premises became **Tynemouth Dene Saw Mill and Cooperage Limited** and then later in 1901 the Electricity Works. The tannery is shown on the maps of Fryer 1722 and Wood 1827.

This photograph shows Dene House on Tanners Bank which was the only building left of the Tanning Works in the 1900's. The official address for Tanners Bank was Low Lights and as John Richardson was known to reside at "Low Lights" this may well be the house he built in 1766.

It is known to have been still occupied in 1947 but there is no record on the 1950 Electoral Register so it must have been unoccupied or demolished around that time.

When John Richardson died in 1800 his son Henry inherited the tannery and as he and his wife had no children, they adopted Henry's nephew John Richardson Proctor born in 1813 (son of Joseph Proctor and Henry's

sister Elizabeth) who on the death of Henry in 1834, became the third owner of the tannery. In the 1841 census John Richardson Proctor aged 28, resided at the Low Lights as a master tanner employing 10 men. In 1867 he moved to the villa "Clementhorpe" which he had built at Preston Park and he and his wife Lydia had a son in 1850 named Henry Richardson Proctor and in the 1871 census he is listed living at Clementhorpe employing 26 men and a boy.

Pew Dene Tannery 1780

The premises of Ogilvie and Son, **Magnesia and Salt Manufacturers** on the Ropery Bank were advertised for sale in the North and South Shields Gazette of 6th September 1855. Joseph Ogilvie Snr died 1850 and in the 1881 census Joseph Ogilvie, born North Shields in 1811, is mentioned as a retired salt manufacturer of Rosella Villa, Preston. With an entrance on Ayres Terrace this was Rosella Hall House on the area of land where Springfield, Ashfield Grove and the Health Centre now stand. He lived here from 1876 until his death in 1895.

The **Low Lights Pottery** situated behind the Low Light, owned by John Carr b. 1801 was first mentioned in a trade directory of 1834. His son Thomas William Carr b. 1835 rented four acres in Spital Dene and built the greenhouses which existed till 1988. In 1858 the company's name changed to John Carr and Sons when his sons Thomas and Robert joined the company. By 1881 they employed 72 men, 45 women and 21 boys, producing all manner of fine domestic pottery much of which was exported to the Mediterranean, India and Egypt. The pottery manufacture ceased with a public auction sale of the plant and all associated machinery and moulds on the 30th March 1894 although they continued in the manufacture of glazed bricks and similar items until around 1910.

The **North Shields Lime Works** is shown on Woods plan of 1826 built on land owned by Collingwood and Partners. Lime and coal was carried here along the Whitley Waggonway to the east of Tanners Bank and along the west side of Clifford's Fort to the Low Lights Staiths from Whitley Quarries and Cullercoats Main Colliery. The line was abandoned in 1848.

The lime kiln, crushing mill and whitening works (where lime was made into a bleaching agent) may have prompted the development of the Iron Foundry on adjoining ground to the north and east, since lime could be used as a flux in iron and steel making. It was also an important commodity in the tanning industry. The lime kiln is shown on the first edition of the Ordnance Survey map (1857) but by the second edition, this area was occupied by North Shields Glazed Brick Works and Flint Mills.

North Shields Guano and Fish Oil Works was established here by W S Corder in 1888 on previously undeveloped ground north of the brewery and west of the Pow Burn. The chemical works expanded and in 1892 another square building was added. In 1901 the premises were occupied by the Tyne Brand Company which began by canning herring and later various tinned foods.

The **Low Lights Tavern** at the bottom of Brewhouse Bank was situated on the side of the burn and is probably the oldest Public House that is still trading in North Shields. It is suggested there has been a public house on the site for about 400 years.

The Dene took the name Spital Dene from **St Leonards Hospital** which was situated between the two branches of the Pow Burn in the centre of what is now Northumberland Park. The park and Tynemouth Golf Course are separated by the embankments, which carry Tynemouth Road and the Newcastle to Tynemouth Railway and King Edwards Road respectively.

Looking west over the congested Pow Burn Dene in 1830.

Before the building of these roads the Pow Burn ran from near Preston Village to the River Tyne and was navigable for some distance towards the present Tynemouth Road. A plaque on the wall near the Tynemouth Lodge Hotel marks the site of the "**Governor's Tree**" which was where important visitors to Tynemouth were met as they disembarked in Pow Burn. These visitors included King Charles I in 1633 and King Henry VIII's commissioners when they came to dispossess the Monks of Tynemouth Priory in 1539. When the Black Friars monastery was dissolved on the 10th June 1539 the fabric of the buildings was used to build the Low and High Lights on the banks of the Pow Burn.

An article in the local press dated 14th February 1861 alludes to the earlier size of the Pow Burn when mentioning the new Railway Station behind the Tynemouth Lodge Hotel as follows:

"Excavations for the Blyth and Tyne Station near the Master Mariner's Asylum Tynemouth unmistakably revealed a period long anterior to the earliest traces of civilisation, when the north mouth of the Tyne had communicated with and covered the whole of the

15

embankment east and west of the Dene, as far North as the ancient hospital, which stood for centuries in Spital Dene. The cemetery which existed in the 16th century at the west side of the Dene, must have been formed long after the tidal wave had ceased to reach the altitude of the banks."

King Henry VIII gave the Trinity House a charter to build and embattle two towers at the entrance to the haven of the River Tyne which would burn a candle every night for incoming ships to navigate by. In 1658-9 the stone structures were demolished and replaced by timber structures that could be moved to allow the lights to be moved corresponding to the movement of the sand banks in the river.

The southern end of the Pow Burn was culverted and flows into the Tyne at **Peggy's Hole,** named after the anchorage site where the Press Gang Warship the "Peggy" moored. It is recorded that on 26th April 1793, 250 mechanics and seamen were pressed into service here during a raid when the town was cordoned off by the regiment from Tynemouth barracks enabling press-gangs from various armed vessels in Shields harbour to force these men on board the ships.

The event immortalised in the song:

Here's the Tender Coming

Here's the tender cominn' pressing all the maen
Oh, my hinny, what shall we de then?
Here's the tender comin' off at Shield's bar
Here's the tender comin' full of men-o'-war.
Hide me bonnie Geordie hide yersel away
Wait until the frigate makes for Druridge Bay
If they tyek yer Geordie whes te'win wor breed ?
Me and little Jackie would be better off deed.

They always came at night, they never came at day
They always came at night to steal your lad away
Here's the tender coming full of red marines
Here's the tender coming, ye kna what it means.

On the eastern side of the Pow Burn a fort was built in 1672 to replace a much more basic fort of 1642. This was to defend the River from enemy warships during the Third Anglo-Dutch War of 1672-1674 and was named **Clifford's Fort** after Lord Clifford of Cabal. It was designed by a Swedish military engineer, Martin Beckman; built by a Yorkshire architect, Robert Trollope and was built on a raised platform, surrounded by walls with a three storey redoubt at its centre which housed the Governor's apartments, a gun powder magazine and an armoury. It was irregular in shape with its long axis running north to south and protected by a low riverside gun battery of 20, 20 pound and 10, 10 pound cannons with its main gateway at the north end, the natural channel of the Pow Burn defending the land side and was under the command of the Governor of Tynemouth Castle until 1839.

It enclosed the Old Low Light which was built between 1717-1733 and extended in 1777. Its white gable end was painted black as it is today and its light window blocked to obscure it as a navigational landmark when converted to almhouses in 1806-8 after the New Low Light was erected by Trinity House.

In 1881 the fort was declared obsolete but in 1888 was recommissioned as the headquarters of the Tyne Division Royal Engineers (Volunteers) Submarine Miners. Most of the old buildings were demolished to make room for new buildings and the old gun placements blocked. A narrow

gauge railway was laid to carry mines to boats from a new gate in the south east angle and defended with two new gun placements.

In 1928 the Fort was again decommissioned and handed over to Tynemouth Corporation to use for the expansion of the fishing industry. The present surviving west and north walls of stone rubble beneath brick parapets, with gun ports and musket loops are remnants of the 1672 fort which throughout its history never actually witnessed action with a foreign enemy except when in 1941 the Lifeboat House to the east was destroyed by a German bomb.

On the southeast boundary of Northumberland Park next to the site of the Governor's Tree is situated the former **House of Correction** and Justices Room for the Parish of Tynemouth. It was decreed at the Christmas Sessions at Morpeth on the 13th January 1789 that a House of Correction was required at North Shields and Thomas Fenwick and Thomas Bigge were authorised to find a suitable location. They reported at the Easter Sessions that they had found a site on the Powebank near to Lowlight Farm belonging to John Walker of Dockwray Square and were instructed to purchase the site for a sum not exceeding £45. The Correction House was duly built in 1792 and later the **Tynemouth Lodge Hotel** was built for William Hopper and has been trading as a public house since 1799. William Hopper was listed in 1855 as still being the publican at the Tynemouth Lodge. A tunnel linked the two buildings to supply food from the hotel to the prisoners.

The Correction House was a prison comprising of fourteen cells, for minor offenders such as prostitutes, as more serious offenders were sent to the County Gaol at Morpeth, where hangings took place. The 1841 Census recorded James Robb aged 50 as Governor and his wife also aged 50 as Matron assisted by three Residents looking after 24 prisoners. Circuit Judges regularly stayed at the Tynemouth Lodge Hotel, whilst presiding at the Justices Room which was the local court house. On the occasion of the Golden Jubilee of King George III on the 25th October 1809 it is recorded that the prisoners were given a good dinner and a quart of ale on the order of the Magistrates. There are recorded two escapes from the prison, William

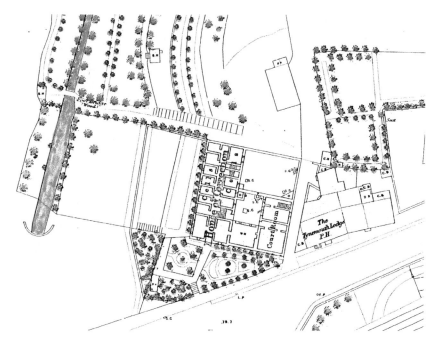

Correction House from 1857 10 inch Ordinance Survey map showing the 14 cells and extensive gardens.

Daglish escaped on the 26th July 1885 and on 2nd April 1886 Arthur Henderson escaped by scaling the wall of the exercise yard but was recaptured.

Of the hundreds of Houses of Correction built by order of Parliament in the eighteenth century this is one of just a few remaining and was designated a Grade 11 listed building in 1999. In 1907 the building was purchased by The Tynemouth and District Laundry Co Ltd which became The Superb Cleaning and Valeting Service Ltd from 1961 until its closure in 1968. The Plastix and Metal Engraving Co Ltd occupied the building from 1990 until 1994.

Two of the original cell windows are still visible on the west wall facing the Park playing field.

19

The Tynemouth Lodge Hotel, which had fallen into disrepair and was threatened with demolition was restored by Hugh Price in the 1980's and is now a very popular free house specialising in draught beers and lagers.

An article in The Tyne Mercury dated 17th October 1815 stated "On Michaelmas-day, the new road from Tynemouth Castle gates to Newcastle, over Pow-dean Mound (a large mound of earth recently laid across a deep valley, near Tynemouth Barracks), was opened for carriages; and now coaches and gigs travel almost in a direct line from Byker Hill to Tynemouth, shortening the distance considerably. From the fourth milestone, near Wallsend the road goes upon the ancient Roman Line, nearly to Tynemouth Cliffs, where the several cohorts of the third legion were stationed, some centuries before the building of the Priory or Castle. On cutting down the swell of the bank on the west side of Pow-dean, alias Spittle Dean, the workmen came to some remains, appearing as if camp fires had once been there."

In the Tyne Pilot Magazine during 1839 various letters were published on the suggestion of providing public gardens in Spital Dene. Suggestions were proposed for the area from "The Mound to the north hedge to create serpentine walks interspersed with seats, arbours and grottos, with basins, fishponds, fountains and a large greenhouse in the centre". The Editor replied on the 21st

September that they would like to see the "whole of the valley from the Correction House to Spital Dene Bridge, together with the little hollow running up to Raeburn's Farm and Codling's Cottage laid out in the style spoken of – while on the irregular ground between, on which the hospital formerly stood – there should be a building for refreshments etc."

Another letter stated that "the whole of the valley was filled with copse wood but about forty years ago had been grubbed up and the valley converted into a garden which although very productive, was neglected and became what it is today, a mere waste." However when the park was created in 1885, 3.75 acres in the northwest corner was still known as Mrs M Morris's garden and Mr Robert Cornfoot Carr who had maintained 4 acres including two greenhouses, workman's cabin, croquet lawn and a vinery and a peach house in the centre of the dene had them incorporated into the park.

Mr Robert Carr had looked after these gardens from 1867 when his brother Mr Thomas William Carr emigrated to Australia and left them in his care until 1884. Mr Thomas Carr had rented these 4 acres from 1862 and had laid out gardens and built a workman's cabin and the two large greenhouses which remained until demolished in 1988 still with the original tiled floor. In front of the greenhouses he created a croquet lawn and planted a hawthorn tree which was removed about the same time as the greenhouses.

One of Thomas William Carr's sons Stanley, who returned to England remarked in 1934 "the hawthorn tree

Mr Carr's Workman's Cabin and Greenhouse from 1860's pictured in the 1920's with an aviary behind the Greenhouse.

that Father planted is still going strong and the cabin where afternoon teas were held and sundry things and is still used by the Council Gardeners".

This magnificent hawthorn tree can be seen in the bottom left corner of the picture below which I took in the early autumn of 1972.

The first lease for **Spittal Dean Farm** was from the 15th March 1784 for 20 years at a rental of £132.00 per annum. The actual document shown states:
"The Dwelling House or Farm House, stablebyre, barn and granary all newly erected and built by the said Ralph Codling and several closes or parcels of land called Pond Close, Little Spital Close, North Bank, Bank Field, Wayfield, Pasture Close, Pond Field, North Pit Hole Close, West Gells Close, East Gell's Close and Spittal Yards containing

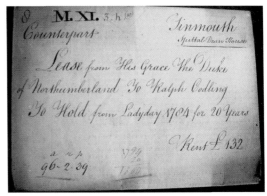

This Indenture, Made the *Sixteenth* Day of *March* in the *Twenty fourth* Year of the Reign of our Sovereign Lord *George the Third* by the Grace of GOD, of Great-Britain, France, and Ireland, King, Defender of the Faith, and so forth; and in the Year of our LORD one *Thousand Seven Hundred and Eighty four* **Between** The Most Noble Hugh, Duke and Earl of Northumberland, Earl Percy, Baron Warkworth of Warkworth Castle, Lord Lieutenant and Custos Rotulorum of the Counties of Middlesex and Northumberland, of the City and Liberty of Westminster, and of the Town and County of the Town of Newcastle upon Tyne; Vice-Admiral of all America, and of the County of Northumberland, one of the Lords of his Majesty's most Honourable Privy Council, and Knight of the Most Noble Order of the Garter; of the one Part. **And** *Ralph Codling of Spittal Dean in the County of Northumberland Yeoman* ————

———— of the other Part, **Witnesseth** that, for and in Consideration of the Rents, Covenants, and Agreements, herein after referred, mentioned, and contained; and, on the Part and Behalf of the said *Ralph Codling his* Executors, Administrators, and Assigns, to be paid, performed, and kept; He the said Duke of Northumberland **Hath** granted, demised, leased, set, and to Farm let; and by these Presents **Doth** demise, lease, set, and to Farm let, unto the said *Ralph Codling All those Lands and Tenements in Tinmouth in the said County consisting of the several particulars herinafter mentioned that is to say a Dwelling House or Farm House, Stable Byer, Barn and Granary all newly erected and built by the said Ralph Codling and now commonly called or known by the name of Spittal Dean House, — And also the several Closes or parcels of Land called Bond Close, Little Spittal Close, North Bank, Bank Field Wayfield, Pasture Close, Pondfield North Pithole Close, West Gills Close, East Gills Close, and Spittal Yards containing together ninety six acres, two roads and thirty nine perches the same more or less now in the possession of the said Ralph Codling and Cuthbert Hopper.*

together ninety six acres, two roods and thirty nine perches in the possession of Ralph Codling and Cuthbert Hopper."

The following are later leases for the farm: 1809 William Tate, 1815 Thomas Robson, 1816 and 1833 Robert Raburn (died 1838), 1842 James Raeburn, 1845 C.H. Laws, 1851 George Nellis, 1884, 1885 and 1908 Henry Christopher Nelless then 1913 Tynemouth Golf Course.

Spital Dean or Raeburn's Farm is shown on John Wood's map of 1826 and on the 1841 census **Spital Dene Farm** was occupied by James Raeburn aged 50 (a farmer of 23 acres) along with his wife and three daughters and two servants. In the 1851 census James Raeburn aged 59 is recorded as a widower with only two daughters at **"Lodge Farm"**, his third daughter Elizabeth now Wallace resides with her husband and one month old son in the **"Outhouses"** at the farm. These records obviously refer to the same farm buildings.

In the 1841 census at **Manor Mill** is recorded Christopher Nelless aged 50 Miller/Farmer with son George aged 30 an agricultural labourer and eight other members of family and workers.

In the 1851 census at **Tynemouth Mill** (presumably the same building, as there is no mention in this census of Manor Mill) is recorded George Nelless aged 40 head farmer with his wife Hannah, sons Henry aged 2 and John Thomas aged 1 week, along with 2 servants.

The 1861 census records Henry aged 52 with wife Hannah and 6 children now at **Spital Dene Farm** but the

1871 census records Hannah Nelless there as a widow with 3 sons – Henry C aged 22, John aged 20, William aged 16 and 1 daughter – Hannah aged 12 along with 2 farm servants.

The 1881 census lists Henry C Nellis (different spelling) as the head of the household farming 68 acres with "two clowns and a boy". (Clown being old English for a peasant.)

From 1883 until 1890 William Nelless and from 1891 until 1901 Henry Christopher Nelless were recorded at Hawkey's Farm which was where Hawkey's Lane School is now situated. However Henry at least returned to Spital Dene Farm as an interesting article appeared in the Shields Daily News of 1st August 1905 of Henry Nelless (who would then be 56 – the son of George) being charged with horse-whipping 13 year old William Wilson Tagg and others for stealing turnips! Henry Nelless and his wife (also Hannah) ran the Farm until they died in 1913 and 1912 respectively. Then in the Shields Daily News of 12th April 1912 it was reported that Tynemouth Golf Course acquired Spital Dene Farm for use as a golf course.

West and East facing sides of remaining farm cart shed, sty and byre.

There are records of there being **Rifle Ranges** in Spital Dene (location unknown) as The Shields Daily News of 11th April 1868

mentioned the 3rd Battery Northumberland Artillery Volunteers held a competition in the Dene and the same newspaper mentioned on 21st September 1869 there was a friendly competition between Non-Commissioned Officers of the 98th Foot and the 1st Northumberland Artillery Volunteers on Saturday at the Spital Dene Ranges.

In November 1878 the Duke of Northumberland offered 10 acres of the Dene to create a park but this was refused due to objections from members of the local authority. The Duke is recorded at being none to happy and considered "washing his hands of the whole business". At this time Alderman John Foster Spence saw the park proposal as an opportunity to provide desperately needed work for the local workforce as well as providing a valuable amenity and started a campaign for the Park. He approached the Duke to persuade him to donate 10 acres for the project and as a result on the 6th October 1879 the minutes of the Parks Committee recorded letters from Mr Snowball, a representative of the Duke again offering the land.

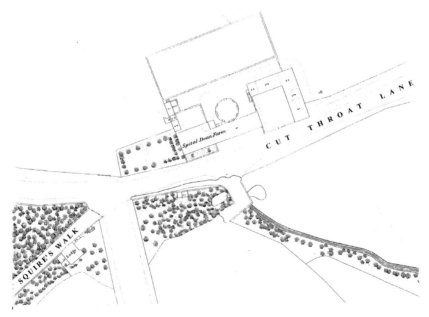

Raeburn's / Spital Dene Farmhouse and showing the Pow Burn and the start of the Squire's Walk and entrance gates and Lodge which led to Tynemouth Lodge, the residence of Colonel Linskill.

The existing recreation ground at the corner of Washington Terrace and Tynemouth Road was included as agreed by the Council.

Council minutes of 24th March 1880 recorded that excavations were in progress at Correction House Bank to widen the road from Tynemouth Lodge to Washington Terrace.

It is recorded that compensation was paid to the following tenants who had to vacate the dene to enable the creation of the park.

Wm Hewison	Rope Works
Mrs Middleton	Stable and land
S Wharton	Tripe House and garden
T W Carr	Cottage, Greenhouse and gardens
T C Storer	garden
Wm Linskill	Grassland in north west corner.

The northwest corner of the park was initially rented from the Duke and the northeast section bordered a garden belonging to Mrs Hannah Morris who is recorded in the 1871 Census residing only at "Spital Dene" as a gardener aged 69 along with her daughter and grandson. This garden was absorbed into the park in 1886.

This cottage which was used as the first Park Keepers residence before the new house was built on King Edward Road in 1940 and which was demolished in the early 1960's was Mrs Morris's cottage. Permission was obtained from the Duke of Northumberland to replace the original cottage on 23rd September 1862. An article in the Shields Daily News of 1862 read "November 28. In digging for the foundations of a new house in the Spital Dene, Tynemouth, human remains were found, including one complete skeleton and the divided members of several others, some very much charred. It is supposed they were the remains of bodies burnt during the time of the Plague and burned hastily, or the remains of soldiers engaged during the Scottish siege of Tynemouth Castle about 250 years ago".

On a map of 1865 there is a building shown where the Park Keepers Cottage stood bordering Mrs Morris's garden with a path leading down into the garden and this ties in with the mention of Mrs Morris in the 1871 census.

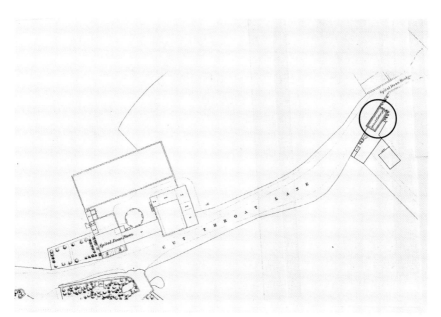

CUT THROAT LANE renamed SPITAL DENE then KING EDWARD ROAD showing position of OLD SPITAL COTTAGE.

This was replaced in 1862 by NEW SPITAL COTTAGE which later became PARK COTTAGE.

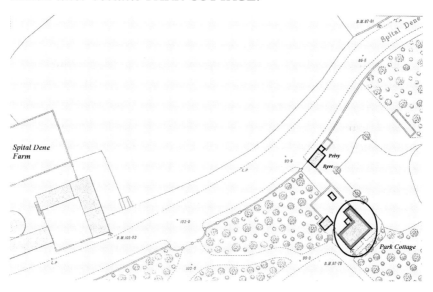

Site of Park Keeper's Cottage with steps where Lion Statues were situated.

EVERYONE HAD TO SIT ON THE LIONS – APRIL 1955.

The Lion Statues were removed and were still in the Council Store in 1991

Park Keeper's Cottage with the Lion Statues hidden behind these lads in their Sunday best in 1959.

Some notes on surrounding streets:

In the Shields Daily News 2nd October 1877 Ald Shotton moved that Cut Throat Lane be renamed Preston Avenue, and the motion was carried.

O/S Map of 1894 shows from Washington Terrace to Holy Saviours Church as Spital Dene Road.

O/S Map of 1913 shows Spital Dene Road now King Edward Road.

In 1922/23 the Council filled in a large amount of Spital Dene to improve the road.

Mariner's Lane was built between 1924 and 1928.

Park Avenue was built in 1905 and was part of Tynemouth Lodge Estate. 20th June 1906 Council Minutes agreed portion of Park Terrace between Kitchener Terrace and King Edward Road be re-named Park Avenue.

Livingstone View was built by John Livingstone Miller in 1886.

St Leonard's Hospital

Spital Dene derived its name from St Leonard's Hospital which was first referred to in an assize roll of 1293 which mentions "the bridge of the hospital of Saint Leonard". The location of the hospital does suggest it may have been a Leper Hospital because of its remote location away from Tynemouth township. Situated on the only road from Newcastle to Tynemouth where the Prior of Tynemouth held markets on Sundays from 1275 meant there would be many people travelling across the Spital Bridge. Medieval Hospitals are known to be quite commonly situated close to bridges which had important symbolic religious connotations and beggars or lepers stationed there could collect alms from all those crossing.

In "Medieval Religious Houses, England and Wales" (Knowles and Hancock 1971) it is suggested that the hospital was founded about 1220. Although there is no record of the hospital's foundation, it was probably dependent upon Tynemouth Priory as it is recorded that Tynemouth Monks supported a leper hospital and as Lord of the Liberty of Tynemouthshire was the principal landowner in Tynemouth Parish.

In 1110 Tynemouth Monastery was rebuilt following its destruction in 1095 by William Rufus the son of William the Conqueror who marched his army to Tynemouth after Mowbray the Earl of Northumbria rebelled against him and

Stone coffins with grave slab in between.

converted the Monastery into a castle to defend his treason.

In this same period in 1112 another St Leonard's Hospital was founded at Mitford near Morpeth by Sir William Bertram in an area still called Spital Hill.

Certain facts suggest a connection with the Benedictine Nunnery of St Bartholomew in Newcastle as Prior Germanus (circa 1141) granted to the Nuns of St Batholomew an annual dole of 8 quarters of wheat out of his granary. Also the Prioress of St Bartholomew held or claimed to hold property in Tynemouth in 1293 and again in 1326/1327 and a contempory list of Monasteries suppressed in 1536 as having incomes under £200 per annum contains the name of the Nuns of Tynemouth.

St Leonard of Limousin (AD 485-560) is believed to have been a Frankish nobleman who decided to follow a religious calling and joined a monastic group at Micy (Orleans). St Leonard became the Patron Saint of prisoners and diseased people and many churches from the time of William I were dedicated to him along with 20 English monasteries and 30 hospitals. Although these were called Leper Hospitals they admitted any who were ill from any sickness.

The word "hospital" derives from the Latin "hospes", meaning a stranger, foreigner or guest. The original function of a hospital was to provide hospitality and shelter for travellers of all kinds, not exclusively for the sick but later a variety of institutions came into being to cater for the poor, the aged and the sick which bore the name "hospital". During the 14th century leprosy became less common in England in fact it has been suggested that the Black Death removed a very high proportion of the sick and reduced the virulence of the disease. Later foundations of hospitals were more in the nature of almshouses catering for the poor and elderly while some of the earlier leper houses changed their function.

In the "Local Records of Tynemouth" Vol 1 (1957) the Rev J Taggart states that in 1320, St Leonard's Hospital and its lands attached was annexed to the Priory of Tynemouth. Like other Leper Hospitals it was built as a result of the Holy Crusades as many of those who had gone overseas and fought in the religious wars contacted a mild form of leprosy which was prevalent throughout Europe in the Middle Ages.

In the "Monastery of Tynemouth" Vol 1 of 1846 by William Sidney Gibson it states that the property of the Prior and brethren at the time of dissolution (1539) prepared for the accounts of the Ministers or Receivers of King Henry VIII demised to Sir Thomas Hilton were lands called "Le Twenty Layes" and 12 "Short Butts" lying in the West Spytell Dene and 6 acres of feeding in the marsh called "Le Lordes Marshe" and also a house called "Le Spytell House" and a close of land there called "Spytell Close" containing 4 acres and 4 acres of arable land lying in the fields there.

The site of the Hospital is referred to in Brand's "History of Newcastle" (Vol.ii.P.91). He states that the ruins in 1789 are still to be traced a little to the west of Tynemouth on the road to Newcastle. The old road to Newcastle went past Holy Saviour Church across the Spital Dene and along Tynemouth Old Road (now called Preston Avenue) to Preston Road, then southwards to Christ Church and from then westwards through the village of Chirton. The present direct road to Tynemouth was not made until after the peace of 1815. Brand refers to Thompson's map of the Manor in 1757, and states that the place where the Hospital stood is called "Spittle Yards", and contained 5 acres, 2 roods and 37 perches. The Spittle was one of the old burial places of the Parish of Tynemouth. The first mention of it in the Parish Records is in 1645. The following is an entry: "It is ordered that the burials shall be in the place appointed for burying, and if any other ground be broken at Spittle to pay to John Cramlington for every burial out of the ordinary place 6d." John Cramlington was one of the Gentlemen of the Four and Twenty in 1645 (an ancient order of notable local men). The first two burials recorded in the Parish Register were in 1656 and 1659 being the two sons of Gabriel Coulson the Parish Clerk. In 1662, 23 burials were recorded and the last recorded at this site was John ffoster of Whitley in 1713/14.

In "A History of Northumberland Vol VIII Tynemouth" published by the Northumberland County History Committee in 1907 it states that the Spital Demense was attached to the little known Hospital of St Leonard. Mention is made in an assize roll of 1293 to the bridge by St Leonards Hospital, a precursor of the modern Spital Dene Bridge. There was at that time no other passage across the Pow Burn for the present Tynemouth Road to Newcastle stopped short at Tynemouth Mill turning south from that point down the eastern side of the dene. On the farther side of the bridge, between the two branches of the burn, the foundations of a medieval building were discovered in 1885 when laying out the Park, though an excavation was not carried out far enough to discover its plan. The building appears to be of considerable size. Its chambers were paved with stone and the few mouldings that remained were of an early English character. Some fragments of flowing window tracery, the base of a cross and the matrix were also found on the spot.

The 15th century stone slab or matrix.

The matrix is a plain limestone slab measuring 5ft 9 inches in length and 2ft 7inches in breadth. It shows indentations which contained brasses of a layman and his wife connected by an inscription fillet. Below these 2 large figures are 5 smaller indents for the brasses of their daughter and 4 sons. The male figures stand on mounds and seem to have worn long loose sleeved tunics, the two females had similar costumes, their hair curled at the side and each had a headdress covered by a kerchief. A date of between 1400 and 1420 has been assigned to the execution of the work.

My interpretation of how the original brasses may have looked.

Two stone coffins were also unearthed in the course of the excavations and a tiled floor about 18 inches to 2 feet from the present surface. The floor was about 20 feet by 12 feet in area and was covered up again to preserve it from any damage. (This reference to the floor was in Mr. H. A. Adamson's account of the Hospital in the Proceedings of the Society of Antiquaries of Newcastle upon Tyne Vol III published in 1889.)

In the 17th century the Hospital was used as a burial ground; it and the Priory appear to have been alternative burial grounds, for in 1603 William Milbank of North Shields left his body to be buried at either of these two places at the discretion of his executors. Many persons were buried here during the Civil War, when in 1645 Parliamentary Forces occupied the castle making burials there impossible.

Captain Linskill, the first Mayor of Tynemouth who lived for a while at Tynemouth Lodge informed Mr. H A Adamson that in the early 1800's the gravestones and monuments from the Spital Yards were removed and broken up and used for "road-metal" when Preston Avenue was relaid in 1815. Then until the Park was created the area was pasture land.

In 1926 William S Garson produced a booklet entitled "The Origin of North Shields and its Growth". Its opening paragraph read as follows: "Entering the Northumberland Park, by the gate opposite the entrance to the golf course, one cannot fail to perceive the remains of St. Leonard's Hospital, which the Tynemouth Monks kept for lepers, and from which Spital Dene is named. This same spot was also once a recognised burial place. Early in the last century the gravestones were removed and the land became pasture. So it remained until Northumberland Park was laid out in 1885, when many stones were unearthed which, no doubt, were the remains of the hospital. Among the relics found were several skeletons, two stone coffins, and a stone slab of the early 15th century.

On the slab are the impressions of a man and a woman and their five children – four sons and a daughter. The brass figures themselves are gone, but the rivets by which these figures were once fastened to the stone may still be seen, the whole slab being in good state of preservation".

In 1539 when Tynemouth Priory was dissolved Spytel

House and Spytal Close were surrendered to the Crown. The land was then leased to Sir Thomas Hilton by King Henry VIII for a term of 21 years. This land eventually passed to Algernon the tenth Earl of Northumberland in 1637.

In a Terrier of 1649 the extent of the Hospital demesne was given as 13 acres, 3 roods, 5 perches lying in 46 rigs and various corners of land in Tynemouth and Preston as well as certain lands in Chirton.

In January 1968 a complete skeleton and three skulls were unearthed by corporation gardeners near the remains of the Hospital.

In 2011 as part of the heritage strategy for Northumberland Park forming part of the "Parks for People" project being part of North Tyneside Council's application for £2.2 million from the Heritage Lottery Fund to enhance the park, an archaeological survey took place to provide information for the restoration plans.

At the request of North Tyneside Council the New Friends of Northumberland Park helped advertise and organize a public meeting held on March 17th in the Linskill Centre, Linskill Terrace, North Shields at which Tyne and Wear County Archaeologist Dave Heslop gave a talk attended by approximately 230 people about the history of the hospital. He outlined the plans for a community archaeology research project with trial trenching in the summer to see what remains of the hospital. At the end of the meeting volunteers signed up to assist the project in a variety of ways including digging, research, interpretation and recording the finds.

In May a geophysical survey was carried out by Timescape Surveys who trained and supervised the volunteers to lay out grids using an electronic distance meter before surveying the site using a magnetometer and resistance meter. This survey mapped subsurface anomalies which might indicate the presence of features of archaeological significance. Then using the information produced volunteers supervised by professional archaeologists from The Archaeological Practice Ltd over three weeks in June and July dug five trenches around the known hospital remains and one on buildings known from early 19th century maps near the Spittal Bridge.

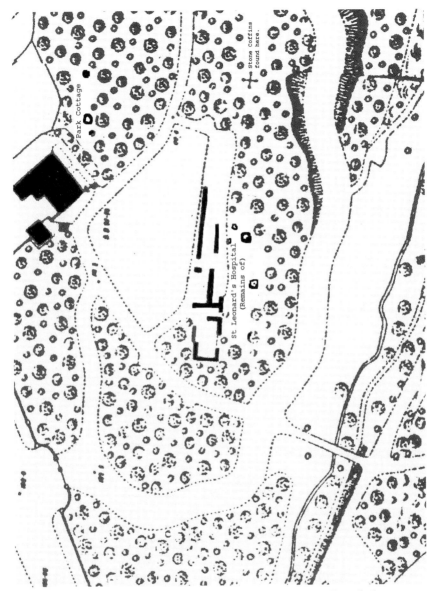

Park Cottage

Stone coffins
found here.

St Leonard's Hospital
(Remains of)

*From a map of 1896 showing extent of the walls of the
Hospital.*

The remains of walls, large cobbles which served as foundations for the walls, paved floor and drains were found, exposed and recorded by scale drawings and photographs. Several medieval graves were uncovered and also a mixture of bones which could represent many more burials, which were probably disturbed when what was a hilly mound was levelled by the Victorians when creating the park. Also found was a considerable amount of pottery, roof and floor tiles but the most interesting finds were a 5000 year old Neolithic stone axe which probably came from a known "axe factory" in the Langdale Valley in the Lake District and a Henry VIII silver penny circa 1520.

Henry VIII Silver Penny circa 1520.

North Tyneside Mayor Mrs Linda Arkley visited the dig and said: "I am absolutely thrilled by the number of people from the community who are involved in this project. The park has come alive again and its heritage will now be a major draw. It is a very special place indeed and the implications of what have been found are very far reaching".

All the finds will be catalogued and recorded and the council will work with local volunteers and the New Friends of Northumberland Park to look for ideas to interpret the history of St Leonard's for today's park visitors. This could include the planting of a medieval herb garden, producing information boards, visitor guides or historic drama events in the park.

A skeleton discovered in 2011 with its arms folded in the 'Christian position'. The remains were not disturbed and re-buried.

Burials at the Spittle

1656	——— son of Gabriel Coulson of Sheels
1658 Jan 6	Gabriel ye sonne of Gabriel Coulson of Sheilds
1662 Mar 29	Thomas Clahanson of Northsheilds
1662 Apr 6	John Cockeram
1662 Apr 6	Roger Davison son of Katharine Davison of Moorhouses
1662 Apr 19	Ralph Pearson of Northsheilds
1662 Apr 21	John Gibson son of Jno Gibson of Gallyhouses near Morton
1662 May 25	Jane Cooper of Northsheilds
1662 June 14	A sea boy yt. lay at Mrs Hockins house
1662 July 27	Matthew Grey of Northsheilds
1662 Aug 4	A child of Mr Edward Tolls
1662 Aug 4	A child of Alexander Curries both unbapt
1662 Aug 5	Sussana d. of Will Metcalfe of Northsheilds
1662 Aug 19	Jno ye S of Morris Johnson Carpenter
1662 Aug 21	George son of Jno Crowfoote of No: shields
1662 Aug 26	Edward son of John Jackson
1662 Aug 27	Margaret d. of ffrancis Davison of No: shields
1662 Sep 10	John Jackson of ye house on Northsheilds bank
1662 Sep 22	Anthony son of Alexander Snawdon of No: shields
1662 Sep 25	Ellinor wife of Jno. Otway of Northsheilds (drowned)
1662 Sep 29	John ye S. of John Hogg of Northsheilds
1662 Sep 29	Margaret d. of Thomas Stones of Northsheilds
1662 Oct 7	John & Anne childr of Alexander Snawden of No: she
1662 Oct 19	A child of William Cocks
1662 Oct 23	Thomas Wilson of Northsheilds
1662/3 Jan 23	James Turner of Northsheilds
1665 May 4	ffrancis Scott
1666 Sep 7	Thomas Gervas belonging to Mr Henry truelove of Ipswitch
1668/9 Mar 24	Allice ye D. of John Ottway
1669/70 Jan 29	Anne Leang
1670 Sep 4	Dame Clapinson
1670 Sep 26	Allice Durham
1673/4 Feb 2	Old John hall of Whitley
1673/4 Feb 12	Margaret wife of John Hall (late of Whitley died at Munckseaton
1674 Apr 27	John Ward of ye low end of Sheilds o poor ffisherman
1675 Oct 29	fisherrnan burried
1675 Nov 24	James Heddon of Preston
1678 Feb 7	James Knocks of Tynemouth

1679 Aug 2   John son of William Dalston
1682 Apr 29   Ralph Wilson of Billy0milne
1684 Aug 28   Geo. Haste of Tinmouth
1684/5 Jan 11 Amye Milburne of Shields
1684 Aug 21   Ann gamsby Widdow
1685 Oct 12   Cuth (or Cath) Johnson of Sheels
1685/6 Mar 8 Issabell Hills (a poor woman)
1686 July 4   Alice wife of James Hebdaigne
1686/7 Jan 6 John Holliss of Shields
1692 May 19   Nicho. Hymars of Preston
1692 Dec 9   Widdow Gamblin of Chirton
1669/700 Jan 14 William Lightley of Sheelds
1705 Sep 18   Tho son of Geo Gibson Salter of Cullercoats.
1707 Feb 6   Jane d. of Antho Elsden of Whitley:
1713/14Feb 23 John ffoster of Whitley

SINGULAR DISCOVERY OF SKELETONS IN NORTH SHIELDS.

During the last fortnight the workmen engaged in the excavations at the new park on Tynemouth Road have unearthed a number of human skeletons, which has given rise to many conjectures as to how they have come there. We understand the number of skeletons found up to the present is about a dozen, each of which have been dug out of a separate grave. It was at first thought that they might be the skeletons of soldiers who fell during battles which were frequent in this neighbourhood, and which took place between the Ancient Britons and Romans about the time of Julius Cæzar, or that they were the remains of some of those who were killed in the time of Cromwell. We learn, however, that the place where they have been found, which is on the top of the bank to the west of the dene, was formerly used as a graveyard; in fact, that it was consecrated and was known as "The Spital Burial Ground." It is therefore probable that the skeletons are those of the earlier inhabitants of Tynemouth, and that they have lain undisturbed for at least 200 years, as it is that time since the last interment took place there. It is expected an effort will be made to have some of the skeletons secured for the museum at the Tynemouth Free Library.

An article in the Shields Daily News of 5th January 1885.

Community Archaeology Research Project – July 2011.

Whitley Waggonway and Blyth and Tyne Railway

The Whitley Waggonway was built in 1811 by Clarke and Taylor to carry coal from Cullercoats Main Colliery to the Low Lights Staiths and Limestone from Whitley Quarries to the North Shields Limeworks. A map of 1757 shows the Pow Burn curving east before the Spital Bridge under the present railway embankment, so this must have been culveted when the wagonway was built. The staiths were situated just to the east of the Low Lights. On a map of North Shields dated 1827 the Whitley Coal and Lime Waggonway is shown running from the Fish Quay and along the present east boundary of the Park, across the present golf course to Whitley Bay.

In 1843 the only outlets for a large portion of the coal producing area of Northumberland were the small private harbours of Blyth and Seaton Sluice. Messrs Jobling and Partners, the lessees of the Cowpen and Hartley Collieries

The remains of the railway with only a few sleepers still visable. Looking west with Livingstone View in the background.

wanted to ship coal from the five collieries of Cowpen, Bedlington, Netherton, Bedlington Glebe and Hartley at the Low Lights, North Shields.

It was proposed to run a line directly south from the Blyth to the Tyne coinciding in part of its course with the Whitley Waggonway. In July 1845 Messrs Jobling and Partners decided to construct a part of the proposed railway and by forming a junction with the Seaton Delaval Railway and connecting with the Seghill Railway secured a provisional route to the Tyne.

In August 1845 the works of the Blyth and Tyne Junction Railway as it was called commenced and the line was opened in 1846.

The old coal staiths on the Tyne were taken down in 1850 and this part of the waggonway was abandoned. On the 4th August 1853 the Blyth and Tyne Company applied to construct a branch from Newsham to Morpeth and part of a branch to Tynemouth from New Hartley to the Dairy House near Seaton Delaval.

A deed of covenant dated 30th May 1854 between the Blyth and Tyne Railway Company and The Duke of Portland specified the rates of carriage over his Northumberland Estates to Tynemouth or The Low Lights for the first 42 years of the Way Leave Lease. These were for up to 40,000 chaldrons (a coal wagon holding 53 hundredweight) of round coal – 4 shillings and 4 pence per chaldron and for small coal 3s 8p per chaldron; up to 50,000 chaldrons 4s 2p and 3s 6p respectively and up to 60,000 chaldrons 4s 1p and 3s 5p. Over 60,000 chaldrons would be 4s and 3s 4p respectively. I do not know what were the actual quantities carried.

On 31st October 1860 the line between the Dairy House and North Shields was opened utilizing the old course of the abandoned waggonway, with Spital Dene Bridge carrying the line over Cut Throat Lane and terminating at a station alongside the Master Mariner's Asylum. This station was called Tynemouth Station from 1860 until 1864. An entry in the local press at the time stated "The Blyth and Tyne Railway Company have erected a new station adjoining the Tynemouth Road, and a few yards eastwards of the Tynemouth House of Correction. It is a brick building with stone facings and comprises ladies first class waiting room, general waiting room and booking office."

In 1861 the House of Commons passed a bill enabling the Blyth and Tyne Railway to extend the railway from North Shields terminus to the proposed docks at the Low Lights and in 1864 the line from Seghill was carried forward to a more suitable termination near the North Eastern Terminus Station at Oxford Street, Tynemouth from which it was only separated by the turnpike road. Also in 1864 the Blyth and Tyne Railway was extended from Monkseaton Station to Newcastle via Backworth and terminated at Picton House, designed by John Dobson like the Central Station but a quarter of a century earlier, on the western bank of the Pandon Dene.

The Blyth and Tyne Railway was taken over by the North Eastern Railway Company in 1874 and in 1887 the line was abandoned when the new eastern loop was opened. The track was lifted between Spital Dene Bridge and Marden Quarry but the southernmost section was reused as part of the North East Railway Newcastle, Tynemouth and Newcastle line. Initially it formed a loop with the parallel line until the older line was abandoned, except for a short stretch from Tynemouth Station running under Mariner's Lane giving access to the old Blyth and

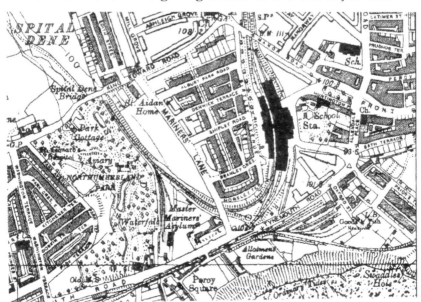

Showing the line to Tynemouth Station passing under Mariner's Lane.

Tyne Railway Station which was used as a Coal Depot. Steam trains still used the line to deliver coal to a depot on the site of the old Tynemouth Station until the closure of the Percy Main Coal Yard in 1966 when coal deliveries stopped after which the depot was demolished and Hazeldene Court was built upon the site.

In June 2010 with funds provided by English Nature a "link path" was created along the route of the railway to join the path at the east of the park to Tynemouth Station passing under the Mariner's Lane bridge. In April 2012 a new entrance was created giving access to the park from the western station car park below Birtley Avenue.

On the parapet of the Mariner's Lane bridge crossing the Old Blyth and Tyne Railway Line can be seen some Victorian carved graffiti. The picture below shows the inscription and on the second picture I have coloured the letters to make it clearer.

How long did it take to chisel this into the stonework?

Jabez Jewitt was born in North Shields in 1841 and until the age of 20 lived in Shotton Colliery and was a miner. By 1871 he was a Railway Signalman and lived most of his life at Percy Square, Tynemouth (where Knotts Flats now stands).

On the 1901 Census his occupation is Nightwatchman and he died in 1911 in Tynemouth Union Workhouse at 50, Preston Road, North Shields.

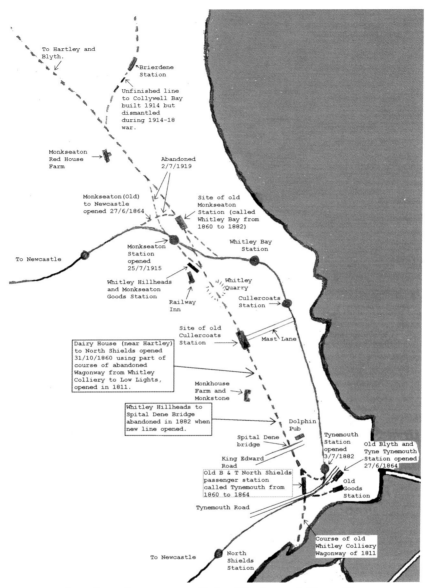

A map showing the routes of the Blyth and Tyne line.

Master Mariner's Home

In 1829 a friendly society The Tyne Mariner's Benevolent Institution was set up to provide pensions for retired ship's masters who were not very affluent in their old age. Shortly after being established a suitable site was sought to erect a building where the Old Masters or their widows might spend their last days.

The Duke of Northumberland was approached and he gave the society the land on the west of the main road between North Shields and Tynemouth. On the opposite side of the road were the remains of the barracks erected in 1756 for the accommodation of 1,000 men and to the west of the site in later years stood the Blyth and Tyne Railway Station.

A foundation stone was laid on 18th October 1837 and a special appeal was made for funds and was so well subscribed that the building was completed by 1840 at a cost of £5,100 consisting of 32 flats each with two rooms.

The Third Duke of Northumberland was succeeded by his brother Algernon Percy in 1847. He was Admiral of the Fleet and also at one time First Lord of the Admiralty and took a great interest in the institution to which he made several handsome donations.

This is the base of the 1840 statue of the 3rd Duke of Northumberland in his ceremonial robes of the Order of the Garter.

Mr C Tate of Newcastle was commissioned to create the statue but died before completion and Mr R G Davies completed the work.

The plaques read as follows:

THIS PLAQUE WAS UNVEILED BY
HIS GRACE THE 12TH DUKE OF NORTHUMBERLAND
ON 7TH JULY 1997
TO COMMEMORATE THE FOUNDING
OF THE
TYNE MARINERS INSTITUTE IN 1897.

TYNE MARINERS' BENEVOLENT INSTITUTION
11TH SEPTEMBER 1937.
THIS TABLET WAS UNVEILED BY HER GRACE
THE DUCHESS OF NORTHUMBERLAND
TO COMMEMORATE
THE CENTENARY OF THE INSTITUTION.

This is the coat of arms of the Master Mariners Friendly Society positioned above the front main entrance. It depicts an anchor with grappling hook above with their motto "Deus Dabit Vela" – God will fill the sails.

Towards the end of the century the financial position of Master Mariners greatly improved and the usefulness of the Master Mariner's Asylum was greatly diminished but on the other hand there were large numbers of ordinary seamen on Tyneside who found themselves without means after their working life. In 1897 "the Tyne Mariner's Institute" had been founded to assist aged and infirm seamen and in 1902 these two institutions amalgamated and became a charitable organisation.

In February 2003 The Durham Aged Mineworkers Homes Association took over the management from the Tyne Mariner's Benevolent Institution and to this day the building which is recognised as a Grade II listed building still houses 30 retired seamen.

Tynemouth Mill and other historical buildings

Believed to be on site of corner of Millview Drive and Algernon Terrace. There had previously been a "Tynemouth Windmill" where the Master Mariner's Home stands but this burnt down in 1805.

1841 Census

Manor Mill	Christopher Nelless	50 yrs	Miller/Farmer
	George "	30	Lab
	Mary "	25	
	Christopher "	22	
	Dorothy "	20	
	Martha "	20	
	Thomas Turner	6	
	Christopher Turner	4	
	Isabella Liddle	19	
	Joseph Milburn	13	Ag Lab

1851 Census

Tynemouth	George Nelless	40	Head Farmer
Mill	Hannah "	28	Wife
	Henry C "	2	Son
	John Thomas Nelles	1week	Son
	Isabella Miller	20	Servant
	John Jordan	13	Servant

The Shields Daily News of 18th May 1903 recorded the death of Robert Tobling Husband of the late Jane Tombling at the Mill House, Spital Dene.

LIVINGSTONE VIEW

Built between 1881 and 1886 by John Livingstone Miller.

Livingstone View and St Aidan's Children's Home after King Edward Road was levelled in 1922.

SPITAL DENE HOUSE / SPITAL HOUSE

Still in existence adjoining The Dolphin Public House.

The building is shown on the 1859 Map.

1881 Census	William Hodge – General Dealer
1887 Burgess Roll records	William Hodge at Spital Dene House
1910 Burgess Roll records	William Laidlow at "Spital Dene Dwelling House"

SPITAL COTTAGE

On 1865 map on Cut Throat Lane (King Edward Road) near Spital Dene Cottage.

1841 Census	Matilda Maddison		90 yrs	Independent
	Theodosia	Surtees	50	
	Caroline	"	25	
	Lionel	"	17	
	Henry	"	16	
	Barnett	"	7	
	Mary Dixon		20	
	Margery Pattison		20	
1851 Census	Dennis Hill		50	Draper
	William Hill		17	Draper
	Chas Dennis Hill		16	Draper
	Henry Alfred Hill		14	Draper
	Sarah Hill		12	At home
	Harwick E Hill		9	Scholar

Plus 3 Visitors and 4 House Servants.

DOLPHIN PUBLIC HOUSE

1841 Census   James Dixon   82 yrs Publican
                  Mary   "   35   Spinster
                  Jane   "   30
                  Isabella "   28
                  James Pyke   25   Independent

1855 John Foster Publican Dolphin at Spittal Hill, Tynemouth.

The Shields Daily News 19th May 1869 mentions a suicide at the Dolphin Inn.

1881 Census   William Dunn 39yrs   Liscensed Victuallarian

1887 Burgess Roll records – William Dunn at Spital Dene Pub

1910 Burgess Roll records – William Dunn at Spital Dene Tenement?

Sept 1959 – Provision of new gate near St Aidan's Childrens Home – known as Dunn's Gate.

SPITAL DENE COTTAGE

1841 Census

Ann Codling	65 yrs	
Liddle Codling	15	Mason

1851 Census

John Lingleter	52	Anchorsmith
Mary "	53	
Nicholas "	29	Anchorsmith
Dorothy "	21	
Elizabeth "	18	Dressmaker
Mary "	15	Dressmaker
Thomas "	11	Scholar
Jane Todd	Mother	Pauper

SPITAL DENE COTTAGE
(This replaced Codlings Cottage)

No cottage is shown on the 1859 Map where the Park Keeper's House stood.

From Shields Daily News 1862: "November 28th in digging for the foundations of a new house in the Spital Dene, Tynemouth, human remains were found, including one complete skeleton and the divided members of several others, some very much charred.

It is supposed they were the remains of bodies burnt during the time of the Plague and burned hastily, or the remains of soldiers engaged during the Scottish siege of Tynemouth Castle about 250 years ago."

On 1865 map there is a building where Park Keeper's cottage stood which borders the south side of "Mrs Morris's Garden".

On 1871 census: In Spital Dene Hannah Morris (aged 69) gardener and daughter and granddaughter.

Tynemouth Golf Club

The Spital Dene Farm had been leased by the Duke of
Northumberland to the Nelles family for many years,
Henry Nelles took over the running after his father died
and farmed until his death in 1912.

As the lease was now for sale Tynemouth Corporation
approached Mr Tuck, the Duke's agent. The lease was on
70 acres including the house and outbuildings at a rate of
£215 per annum. At this time a band of golfing enthusiasts
exploring the possibility of forming a golf club in the
Borough of Tynemouth thought the Spital Dene offered a
natural choice comprising of the farm with arable land and
with the Pow Burn trickling its way through the valley on
the way to the River Tyne. They took over the lease from
the corporation and the Shields Daily News of 12th April
1912 recorded the acquisition of Spital Dene Farm for use
as a golf course.

A public footpath running through Spital Dene Farm to
Preston Village presented a problem but a provisional
committee formed in April 1912, attended a Council
meeting of the Tynemouth Corporation and it was agreed to
divert the footpath while the proposals for the club were
unanimously approved.

One month later a public meeting was held at the Prior
School, Tynemouth by which time negotiations for leasing
Spital Dene Farm were well advanced and the opinion of
Wille Park of Musselburgh, a famous course designer had
been sought.

His proposed plan for a fifteen hole course was so arranged that three additional holes could be added when land became available which the committee hoped to obtain from His Grace, the Duke of Northumberland. The registration of the club was authorised in July 1913 with a membership of over 400 and the Duke of Northumberland was elected president.

World War One was looming and the original plan for 15 holes was restricted to 9 which were completed in May 1914.

Spital Dene Farm Buildings were leased from the Duke for a temporary clubhouse but in 1920 the old cow byre was converted for use as a clubhouse.

The full 18 hole course was completed in 1930 and the present Clubhouse completed in 1940.

The Second World War reduced the course to 15 holes again as the additional land acquired from Monk House Farm was handed back to aid in food production.

In 1954 the course was back to 18 holes after the fields were handed back and new greens laid and the committee seized the opportunity to reopen negotiations for part of Davidson's Hallyard Farm, the site of the new Technical School. Arrangements were completed for adding 15 acres and the limit for extension was reached.

Major alterations to the layout of the course were completed in 1958 and the course is recognised as one of the finest tests of golf in the area and as well as providing an excellent recreational amenity is part of a vital wildlife corridor running from the banks of the Tyne.

Spital Dene Farm.

Creation of Northumberland Park

In 1878 the 7th Duke of Northumberland, Henry George Percy offered the land to the council for the purpose of creating a Public Park after overtures instigated by Alderman Shotton who was then Mayor of Tynemouth. This offer was originally rejected for reasons little known outside of the council but in November 1884 when there was great unemployment in the area Alderman John Foster Spence approached the Duke's agent and persuaded the Duke to renew his offer which he did and this was accepted. Controversy surrounded the employment of strangers to the exclusion of natives as illustrated by a letter published in the Shields Daily News on 4th December 1884 from Mr Robert M. Tate of the Sanitary Committee who described a rush of men to the Borough Engineer's office on the morning of engagement. The figures given to the Committee by the Borough Engineer were out of a total of 101 employed, 84 were married who support 300 children and 17 single, one of whom at least supports an aged mother. The natives numbered 67 and those who are not actual natives of the borough have resided here on an average nearly 16 years and they number 37. Utilising this cheap labour, 101 workmen were employed at the rate of half a crown a day (12 pence) and under the surveillance of Mr Gomoszynski, the Borough Surveyor, paths were cut into the banks of the Pow Burn and were planted mainly with sycamore, a lake was constructed and making the most of the valley that the Pow Burn had afforded, a sheltered park was created and completed in August 1885.

On 11th August 1885 as recorded in great detail in the Shields Daily News, special trains were laid on and local Banks were closed at noon to mark the occasion. Long before the time for the opening ceremony to commence, crowds of people had assembled along the side of the railway on the east side of the Park, which by the time the Duke arrived had considerably increased. There were also present at the north entrance the Mayor, Mr Robert M Tate and Corporation of Tynemouth, Justices of the Peace for the borough and county and the Mayors of Newcastle, Gateshead, South Shields and Jarrow. At 1 o'clock with brass bands, and admission by ticket only, the Duke of

Northumberland accompanied by the Earl Percy and the Reverand H.S. Hicks arrived at the north entrance and was presented with a silver key from J.G. Micheson's Jeweller of Saville Street, inscribed on the front, "Presened to the Most Noble Algernon George Duke of Northumberland" and on the reverse the Borough Arms and motto "Messis ab Altis".

The party then moved down the broad walk and on arriving at the cutting came in sight of the children arranged on the opposite side to represent a crescent, which is the crest of the Percy's. As soon as the Ducal party came in sight the children cheered lustily and each waved a handkerchief, the whole having an imposing effect. They afterwards went through the programme of songs provided for the occasion, under the leadership of Mr. J.R. Cummings, who was subsequently complimented by His Grace on their performance. The Sons of Temperance Band, under the direction of Mr Hoggarth accompanied the singers and played played selections of music on the croquet lawn during the afternoon.

The Mayor on behalf of the burgesses and inhabitants of the

PROGRAMME·OF·PROCEEDINGS

AT THE

Opening of the Northumberland Park,

TYNEMOUTH,

BY HIS GRACE

THE DUKE OF NORTHUMBERLAND, K.G,

LORD LIEUTENANT OF THE COUNTY,

ON TUESDAY, AUGUST 11TH, 1885,

AT ONE O'CLOCK AFTERNOON.

The Opening Ceremony will take place at the North Entrance, Spital Dene.

A GUARD OF HONOR OF THE

TYNEMOUTH ARTILLERY VOLUNTEERS

Will be Mounted at the East Side of the North Entrance.

THE MAYOR AND CORPORATION WILL RECEIVE THE DUCAL PARTY. AN ADDRESS from the Mayor and Corporation of Tynemouth will be presented by the Mayor and read by the Town Clerk. The Mayor will request the Duke to complete his gift of the Park by declaring it open.

THE MAYOR WILL PRESENT A SILVER KEY TO THE DUKE.

The Duke will then proceed through the Park to the ornamental water, opposite to which His Grace will Plant a Tree to be named " THE DUKE'S TREE;" during this ceremony the Children will sing the several Pieces set forth in the Programme.

ALDERMAN JOHN FORSTER SPENCE, Chairman of the Sanitary Committee, will thank the Duke of Northumberland for his kindness in Opening the Park.

The party will then emerge by the South Entrance.

THE WELLESLEY BAND

Will be stationed West of the South Entrance the Duke leaves the Park.

57

Borough thanked the Duke for his generosity. He added that a recreation ground such as he had kindly supplied was one of the greatest and pressing wants of the borough. The poor people of the town had been shut from the fields and until the present they had only the sea shore to visit. His (the Mayor's) heart was very much moved at this generous act, because he knew what a great benefit it would be to the inhabitants at large, and especially to the poorer inhabitants of the borough.

The Town Clerk, Mr. H.A. Adamson then read an address which was then presented to the Duke. The Duke replied that it was of the greatest satisfaction to him that he had been instrumental in co-operation with them in the creation of the Park, which would benefit and promote the physical and moral welfare of the town and he trusted the tradition of the family would continue after his years.

The party then moved down the walk and to the left of the carriage drive, immediately opposite the lake. The Duke then officially opened the Park by planting a Turkey Oak (although it states English Oak on the plaque) Quercus Cerris 12ft high and The Earl Percy, Henry Algernon George Percy, planted a 9ft Mountain Ash, Sorbus Acupara 20 yards further down the main drive.

The proceedings were concluded by the children singing the song (*right*) composed especially for the occasion by Mayor R.M. Tate accompanied by the "Sons of Temperance"

NEW PARK SONG.

(Written expressly for the occasion by R. M. TATE, Esq., Mayor of Tynemouth.)

A thousand children's voices sing,
As greetings to the laggard spring,
All thanks to Him who makes the flowers
To deck our dimpling dells and bowers,

The blushing rose, the lily fair,
The modest, trembling maidenhair,
The emblematic primrose glows,
As in its bosky bed it grows.

The cushioned daisy decks each rill,
Blue bell, and dancing daffodil;
And over all the stately trees
Bend graceful to the passing breeze.

The feathered songsters swell the sound
Of joy and gladness whirling round;
The sun o'er all his mantle flings,
And fills with joy all living things,

Old men and matrons here are grouped,
Young men and maids with arms enlooped;
In rhythmic motion circling round,
The children gambol o'er the ground.

The noble duke with generous heart,
Is here to take a kindly part,
And hand us o'er the bonnie dene,
All sparkling in the sunny sheen,

The thankful people praise their park
And linger in its paths till dark;
Then brazen bands, to close the scene,
Give forth the notes " God save the Queen."

58

Brass Band. The party then proceeded through the Park and left by the south gate for a luncheon at the Grand Hotel, Tynemouth.

There followed an evening of songs performed by The Tynemouth Artillery Band conducted by Colonel Pilter.

An article was printed in the Shields Daily News on 21st April 1886 describing the "Extensions and Improvements" to the Park. It stated that by the end of the month the park will have had an important addition to its area and beauty made to it. Since the Duke opened the park the full portion of the dene was not laid out and beautified and since that time many men have been constantly employed in extending those parts which had not at that time been brought under cultivation. The principal piece of ground which remained was that known as Mrs Morris's garden, lying at the north eastern corner of the park proper and adjoining the Spital Dene Road. This is likely to prove to be one of the most attractive spots in the whole place being sheltered by the high railway embankment on one side and the rising ground leading to the north entrance on the other. The roadway to the north and the trees to the south create a romantic looking glen and lend a seclusion to the place. A cold wind will be softened and tempered and in summer will prove an arboreal retreat sequestered from both wind and sun. A lake has been formed which is always a focal point for all visitors. All along the northern bank of the park improvements are being carried out meanwhile the recreation ground at the extreme south west corner is being brought into shape. It has been levelled and a bowling green formed. It will be enclosed by two fences the outside one to correspond with the iron palisading of the park and the inside one will be of wood. There will be a hedgerow planted between the two. It is intended to have an entrance from the corner of Washington Terrace and Tynemouth Road. The whole of this labouring work is being done by those who couldn't find work elsewhere and would otherwise have been a burden to the ratepayers. The work under the direction of one or two practical gardeners proceeds apace to the evident satisfaction of the many park visitors.

An announcement was printed in the Shields Daily News signed by the Chief Constable that a band would play in the park on Wednesday 12th June 1895 at 6.30pm and that there would be an admission charge of one penny for adults collected by policemen standing at the gates. There followed letters to the paper and meetings of bowlers and friends protesting against the action of the corporation in charging admission to the park. On the evening of the 12th June there had been arranged a competition between Northumberland Club and Gateshead Club and it was argued that it was not common practice to charge admission to other parks and for the Gateshead players after having paid expenses to travel to North Shields and then be charged to enter the park on top of the Green Fees was intolerable. It was reported in the paper on the 13th June that an extraordinary scene took place at the north gates of the park.

On the two previous evenings meetings had taken place to decide on a course of action to protest at the corporation's decision to charge for admission. The members of Percy and Northumberland Clubs along with supporters met at 6.30pm at the corner of Washington Terrace and Linskill Terrace and within a quarter of an hour a couple of hundred objectors had assembled. It was decided the crowd should march to the gates and demand admission but the gates were closed with a posse of police on duty. A few asked courteously to be admitted but Inspector McKenzie said he was instructed not to allow entry without payment. A few suggested to storm the gates but Mr Sutherland suggested they should hold an indignation meeting on the spot and Mr W. Tagg was asked to preside. Speeches were made against the corporation's ruling stating they did not want music only to go to the bowling greens and that the entertainment was only sparsely patronised and the majority of the public didn't want them. It was agreed that a deputation comprising the chairmen and secretaries of Percy and Northumberland Clubs should lay their grievances to the Parks Committee and only those required to take part in the important engagement with Gateshead should enter the park and the majority, having been shut out of their own park departed to Tynemouth for a friendly game with Tynemouth or the Priory.

Subsequently the council conceded it was unlawful to charge admission and entry charges dropped.

A map of the park dated 1896 shows many of the

original features, the two lakes, the southern one having a fountain and a waterfall leading under the main drive and into a stream and small pool with the stream continuing over another small waterfall before going under the main drive again and crossing the present playing field before going into a culvert beside the boundary wall of the House of Correction.

There are three aviaries shown, a large one on the flower bed below the site of the bandstand and two smaller ones on the main drive next to the greenhouse and one against the wall (the remains of which can still be seen) in front of the gardeners cabin from which I remember smoke curling from the chimney during winter months. The gardeners cabin and the two large greenhouses were built in 1862 by Mr Thomas William Carr who previously maintained gardens and a croquet lawn in the dene before the creation of the park.

There were two public drinking fountains, one beside the north bowling green and one on the main drive opposite the southern lake.

Above: Aviaries in 1901 infront of the greenhouse.

Left: Top of south pond with aviary on far left.

Top of south pond with aviary removed late 1920's.

South pond in early 1920's before aviary removed.

Early 1900's with railway fence visible behind the trees.

An ornate flower bed depicting Mayor Gascoigne whose term of office was 1918 - 1919.

Circa 1925 and 1935 as the Bandstand was demolished in 1937.

Staff in 1920's.

The Shelter which was built in 1929.

The original park keeper's cottage was at the north of the park opposite the site of St Leonard's Hospital and had two stone lions lying on pedestals on either side of the steps which led down to the front door. Only these steps now give evidence to the cottages existence which after the new cottage on King Edward Road was built in 1940, was used as a store but after being vandalised was demolished in the 1960's.

During the early years there was a great civic pride in the park and many benefactors presented wildfowl for the lake or birds and monkeys for the aviaries. One councillor in 1897 offered an alligator for the lake! A letter in the Shields Daily News of 5th November 1895 from a Mr J.W. Ponton suggested that one of the monkeys should be stuffed or at least muzzled after having been observed to bite a child's finger almost severing it by the nail after the child put its fingers through the wires. As interest waned the largest aviary was demolished in 1906 and the others in the 1920's.

In 1923 a brochure produced by Tynemouth and North Shields Corporation described the park as follows:

"The phrase, a perfect paradise, may be somewhat hackneyed, but it is at least accurate when applied to this delightful resort. A long valley through which a tiny burn flowed at its own sweet will has been transformed into a veritable "garden of the Lord". Here are shady trees, rustic bridges, tasteful flower beds, smooth patches of turf, fragrant shrubs, well kept paths, banks on whose sides are a mass of colour in the spring and summer, cosy arbours, pretty ornamental lakes on which wildfowl and graceful swans disport themselves, and last, though by no means least, a plentiful supply of seats. There are a number of bowling greens, and band performances frequently add to the many floral and sylvan attractions of this sweet spot."

One of the bands to play regularly in the Bandstand as was
the Victorian fashion was the Garibaldi Brass Band. They
were a South Shields band who are recorded as having
played regularly in South Marine Park, South Shields
between 1895 and 1907 and then disbanded in 1914.

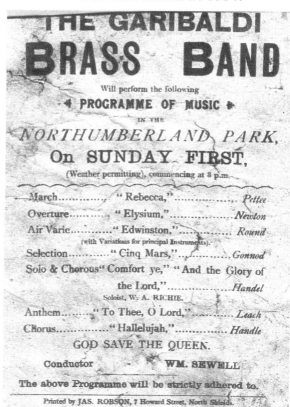

*Unfortunately
the poster shown
here has no date
but presumably
they played in
Northumberland
Park about the
same period as
the photograph
above.*

THE GARIBALDI
BRASS BAND

Will perform the following

♦ PROGRAMME OF MUSIC ♦

IN THE

NORTHUMBERLAND PARK,

On SUNDAY FIRST,

(Weather permitting), commencing at 3 p.m.

March.............. " Rebecca," .... *Pettee*

Overture........... " Elysium," .... *Newton*

Air Varie............ " Edwinston," .... *Round*
(with Variations for principal Instruments).

Selection............. " Cinq Mars," .... *Gonnod*

Solo & Chorus " Comfort ye," " And the Glory of
the Lord," .... *Handel*
Soloist, W. A. RICHIE.

Anthem........ " To Thee, O Lord," .... *Leach*

Chorus............... " Hallelujah," .... *Handle*

GOD SAVE THE QUEEN.

Conductor   -   WM. SEWELL

The above Programme will be strictly adhered to.

Printed by JAS. ROBSON, 7 Howard Street, North Shields.

Park Keepers and Head Gardeners

Compiled from Census Returns and Council Minutes:

1895   G. Taylor, Gardner in Northumberland Park.
        Census return.

1901   George Taylor, Aged 45 Head Gardener – Spital
        Dene. Census return.

19/05/09   George Taylor, Park Keeper gave two weeks notice.
            Then withdrew when promised assistance on summer
            evenings.

19/03/13   George Taylor, Head Gardener at Northumberland
            Park to move to Tynemouth Park at the end of the
            month at a weekly wage of 32s (£1.60p).
            Mr Alfred John Smith Head Gardener at Westend Park
            to transfer to Northumberland Park at a weekly wage
            of 30s (£1.50p).

16/06/15   Borough Surveyor suggested lamplighters could be
            employed as Park Labourers and Park Attendants.

25/10/16   It was agreed 3 women were to be engaged to assist
            the gardeners and the Borough Surveyor was to
            decide as to the amount of wages given.

24/09/19   The Borough Surveyor reported that recently the park
            was largely used as a playground for children doing a
            great deal of damage. Provision made to appoint a
            Park Keeper whose duties are to patrol the park and
            restrain mischievous children.

27/02/24   Staff was to be increased by 1 man bringing the
            summer staff to 8 men and 1 boy.
            It was noted in 1914 there were 10 men and 1 boy.

1924-32   Alfred John Smith, Park Keeper, King Edward Road.
           Voters Register.

27/04/27   The Park Attendant resigned due to illness. The
            gardeners were to undertake his duties on payment of
            overtime.

22/10/30	Mr A Mather, at present engaged at Northumberland Park appointed as Head Gardener under Mr Smith.
1933-39	Robert Mather, Head Gardener, King Edward Road.
21/02/40	New Cottage complete, recommend old Cottage demolished.
31/05/40	Mr Mather promoted to Park Superintendent and vacated the new Head Gardener's Cottage.
06/06/40	Mr Cecil G. Taylor, the Head Gardener, salary £2.16s/week moved into the cottage.
1957	Provision of part time female attendants for school holidays.
Nov 1959	Mr Taylor, Park Keeper retained for one year – now over 65.
Dec 1961	Mr Taylor to vacate cottage after 20 years, now aged 67. Could not get possession of new address till Jan 1963 – service extended to that date.
18/01/63	Mr Arthur T Smith becomes Head Gardner.
1975	Arthur T. Smith, King Edward Road. Voters List.
1977-1989	James Chirnside, Park Keeper. King Edward Road. (Died 24/3/1990, Aged 58)
1990	Future of Park Keeper's House in balance, must remain boarded up until someone employed.
1991	The house was rented to a Council employee who was not involved with the park and this situation was unchanged as at 2012.

Commemorative Trees Planted

The following trees, numbered and positions marked on the following map are known to have been planted with the original inscription plates reading as follows. All of the plates which I believe were of brass have been removed.

1. **"English Oak planted by The Duke of Northumberland on the occasion of the opening of the park. 11th August 1885."** English Oak is in error as it is actually a Turkey Oak (Quercus Cerris). Oak Tree with the Memorial Stone still in situ.

2. **"Planted by the Mayor of Tynemouth Coun William Hutchinson JP. This tree was grown from a chestnut gathered in the ruins of the Place de la Madeline at Verdun in the Autumn of 1918 and was planted here to commemorate the making of peace on the 9th August 1919."** Memorial Stone missing.

3. **"Corporation Planting Committee 1939. Planted to commemorate the Coronation of King George VI by the Mayor of Tynemouth – Coun. A.N. Park."** Ash Tree with the Memorial Stone still in situ.

4. **"Corporation Planting Committee 1939. Planted to commemorate the Coronation of King George VI by the Mayoress of Tynemouth."** Ash Tree with the Memorial Stone still in situ.

5. **"Planted on the 23rd October 1945 by the Mayor of Tynemouth (Coun. Timothy Duff) to commemorate the victorious conclusion of the hostilities in Europe and against Japan during his year of office."** Oak Tree with the Memorial Stone still in situ.

6. **"Planted on the 23rd October 1945 by the Deputy Mayor of Tynemouth (Coun. Robt. A. Anderson) to commemorate the victorious conclusion of the hostilities in Europe and against Japan during his year of office."** Oak Tree with the Memorial Stone still in situ.

7. **"This tree was planted during the Centenary Celebrations by the Mayor of Tynemouth Alderman Richard Irvin J.P. 10th August 1949."** The Tree and Memorial Stone are no longer there.

8. **"This tree was planted by the Chairman of the Centenary Celebrations Committee Coun William Rifle Forster 10th August 1949."** Copper Beech Tree and Memorial Stone still in situ.

9. The Earl Percy also planted on 11th August 1885 a Mountain Ash (Sorbus Acuparia) 20 yards to the south of the Oak. As the Tree and Memorial Stone are missing and the position of the tree as described is where the Shelter stood – was the tree moved when the shelter was built in 1929?

During the Centenary Celebrations three trees were planted at the north end of the main drive overlooking the site of the north lake.

The inscription plates are still legible and from north to south read:

10.

QUERCUS RUBRA
RED OAK
Planted by Councillor B. Flood
Leader of the Labour Group
To commemorate the Centenary of Northumberland Park
11.8.1985

11.

CORYLUS COLURNA
TURKISH HAZEL
Planted by Councillor F.J. Mavin
Deputy Mayor of North Tyneside
To commemorate the Centenary of Northumberland Park
11.8.1985

12.

QUERCUS RUBRA
RED OAK
Planted by Councillor W. Rickleton
Chairman of the Recreation and Amenities Committee
To commemorate the Centenary of Northumberland Park
11.8.1985

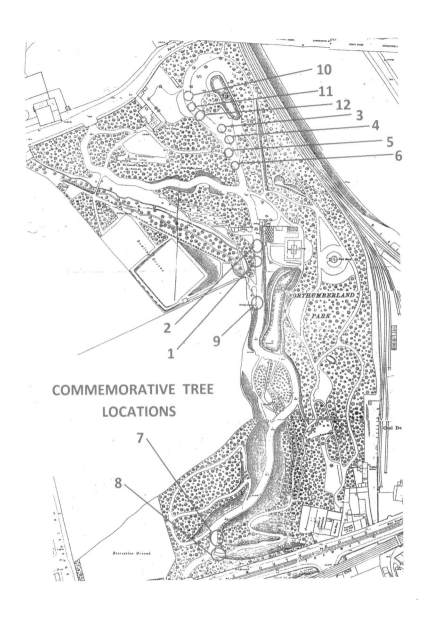

COMMEMORATIVE TREE
LOCATIONS

Above: Commemorative Trees numbered 1 and 2 Turkey Oak and Horse Chestnut.

-THE EVENING NEWS, WEDNESDAY, OCTOBER 24, 1945.

To commemorate victory, the Mayor of Tynemouth, Coun. T. Duff, planted an oak sapling in Northumberland Park yesterday.

Right: The planting of Commemorative Tree number 5 in 1945.

Pet's Cemetery

The Council Minutes of 24th March 1948 recorded a letter received by the Town Clerk from the RSPCA suggesting the council set aside a corner of a public park for the provision of a Pets Cemetery. On the 23rd March 1949 the layout for grave spaces was approved by the Council.

The Pet's Cemetery in the North West corner was founded by Councillor Gilbert Park.

The RSPCA erected a tombstone for "Pop" an Alsatian that saved many lives in Italy during the Second World War where he was used to detect landmines. He was demobbed with leg wounds then was found dead at the foot of Cullercoats cliffs near his home in January 1949. Next to his grave is "Nigger" a Dunkirk veteran and mascot of a Mine Sweeper based at Albert Edward Dock, North Shields. He was later adopted by the Dock Police and ended his days in Whitley Bay Dogs Home in December 1951.

On the 29th May 1954 a deer fawn called Bambi which had been cared for by the RSPCA was buried.

In 1962 the cost of internment was increased to 12/6d as it had been 10/6d since 1948.

Records in 1966 showed 600 pets buried there at a cost of 12/6d to bury a pet and 7/6d for a headstone. Only stones were allowed and not crosses so as not to affect the dignity of the cross.

210 Headstones were still in situ in 2012.

Birds of Northumberland Park

113 Species of which 36 are known to have bred

Some of the earlier records of species recorded here may now seem surprising but it must be remembered how much the environment has changed. Most of the trees have matured creating a dense tree canopy which by blocking out natural light has resulted in a reduction of the shrub and ground flora. An extreme example of a change of habitat can be seen in the area adjacent to Park Terrace down to the main drive which now has the allotments on the bank top and the banks are now heavily overgrown and covered by brambles. Previously this area was open grassland with just a few small trees and shrubs on its slopes and was known as the "Top Field" and where back in the 1940's a local dairyman grazed his ponies. Until the early 1970's this grassland was maintained as such and was scythed every autumn providing an ideal habitat for both small passerine birds and Field Mice and Short Tailed Field Voles and consequently was frequented by hovering Kestrels.

Mute Swan *Cygnus olor*
A pair were present until 1959 (Peter and Mary) when one was killed by vandals and the other died soon after. They had reared young most years. One flew low over the Park on 20th February 2004 and another on 10th January 2006.

Whooper Swan *Cygnus cygnus*
Thirteen in "V" formation flew north low over the treetops on 18th April 2006.

Grey Lag Goose *Anser anser*
Two flew low S-N over the tree tops and dropped towards the pond but didn't land on 26th March 2000. Three also seen flying low going West on 31st March 2001. During a period of extremely cold weather at the end of November 2010 skeins of between 90 and 250 were overhead flying south with over 600 counted on the morning of the 27th.

Mandarin *Aix galericulata*
A gorgeous male was present from 6th to 8th June 2011 and presumably the same individual returned on the 18th September and remained until 25th October during which time it was photographed by numerous visitors to the park.

Wigeon *Anas penelope*
A handsome drake flew in on the 4th October 1964 and stayed for a few weeks.

Teal *Anas crecca*
One was present for a few days from 5th September 1965. During 2004 winter (date unrecorded) four flew over the pond with one breaking away and landed but was attacked by a Moorhen and flew off. One seen in December 2010 during heavy snow.

Mallard *Anas platyrhynchos*
Normally present. During October 2005/April 2006 an unusually large number of 27-30 present. During April pairs were wandering throughout the Park seeking nesting sights and on 18th April I found feathers and the wing tips of a female in the north-east corner which appeared to have been taken by a fox.

Nine ducklings were present on 19th April 2007 and 20 birds present 6th November 2007. Nineteen ducklings were present 4th June 2008 but none were raised in 2009 although 16 birds were here in March. Two broods totalling 19 were hatched in 2010 and one brood of 12 in 2011.

Pintail *Anas acuta*
A male was present for 1/2 weeks in August 1974.

Shoveler *Anas clypeata*
One was present from 24th to 29th September 1972
following strong N.E. winds

Pochard *Aythya ferina*
A female was present for two weeks in October 1974 and a
female was seen on 25th June 2002.

Tufted Duck *Aythya fuligula*
One present during the winter of 1972 and a pair were
seen flying in late evening 15th May 2001. They were very
nervous but started diving for food immediately. I looked
early next morning but they had moved on. On 21st July
2002 a female with 4 day old chicks appeared on the pond,
3 chicks and the female were still there on 4th August. One
young and the female flew away towards the end of August
and the remaining 2 young were last seen on the 3rd
September. Early on 26th October 2009 a female was
present but flew off when disturbed. Another female was
present from the 4th till the 16th December 2010. A pair
flew in on the 7th June 2011 but were gone the next day.

Scaup *Aythya marila*
An unusual record of this essentially "sea duck" when an
adult male, noticeably weak, arrived in stormy weather on
the 1st November 1963. It was caught and ringed on the
4th and flew away on the 10th.

Goosander *Mergus merganser*
One male was seen and photographed on 20th January
2009 but flew off later that same day.

Red Legged Partridge *Alectoris rufa*
One seen by the Park Warden early in 2005 flying low over
the road from the Golf Course and landing inside the Park.

Grey Partridge *Perdix perdix*
Occasional sightings in the late 1970's believed to be birds
from the adjacent Golf Course where there were 8-10
resident at that time. One was flushed by a dog walker in
early April 2009.

Pheasant *Phasianus colchicus*
There were single birds seen in 1972 and 1974 and on 8th April 2004 I saw a female fly over from the Golf Course and land in the dene by the Pet's Cemetery. One male was seen in the same area on 21st October 2005. A female was seen on three dates in early October 2006. A pair were seen on 20th March 2009.

Little Grebe *Tachybaptus ruficollis*
One wintered in 1970 and one stayed for at least a week in early November 1975. I saw a very nervous bird early morning on 10th November 2004, the Park Wardens had noticed it the previous day and it was gone on the 11th.

Cormorant *Phalacrocorax carbo carbo*
Seen occasionally flying over the park, four on the 10th November 2010 were particularly low. One was present on the pond for a week from the 10th January 2011.

Little Egret *Egretta garzetta*
A juvenile was seen on 15th, 17th and 18th July 2001 causing great interest. The same bird was seen in Marden Quarry in the same period when a few were seen on the East Coast.

Grey Heron *Ardea cinerea*
A sighting of a tired bird seen on 26th December 1976 but gone the next day. In the last two weeks of January 2004 an immature bird was seen regularly early in the mornings in the pond or on nearby trees flying away when disturbed. Possibly the same individual seen early morning flying away on 19th February and was wading by the island early morning of 26th February 2004. Presumably the same bird seen frequently in March and up to 8th April becoming noticeably more approachable.
    Early morning Dog Walkers have told me they have

"regularly" see a Heron in the pond throughout 2004/9. I saw one flying over on 6th November 2007.

Sparrow Hawk *Accipiter nisus*
Until recent years there were only four records. Since 1999 two pairs have nested in the locality and one can usually be seen on every visit to the Park. On 12th March 2000 I saw one just miss a Mistle Thrush by the Bowling Greens and in October saw one unsuccessfully attempting to "snatch" a Wood Pigeon from the very top of a Sycamore.

A pair were seen feeding newly fledged young in July 2002 and again in 2003 four young were seen near the bowling greens being fed by two adults. Single birds seen on most days in 2004-2005 twice chasing Great Spotted Woodpeckers. A pair nested near the Bowling Greens in June 2006 but deserted the nest after about 4 weeks incubation. Three were displaying over the park on 16th March 2007 and two displaying on 29th March 2008 but no nesting confirmed. In 2010 a pair nested in May, young were seen in the nest on 28th June and 3 or possibly 4 young flew at the end of July. On 8th March 2011 a pair were seen displaying near last year's nest but nested on the Golf Course.

Buzzard *Buteo buteo*
Two were watched circling over the Park heading South on 28th November 1972 and were seen again the next day. On 19th March 2000 two were seen low over the trees, circling higher and higher then heading off North West. One overhead on 1st August 2009 being mobbed by crows.

Kestrel *Falco tinnunculus*
In the 1960's and early 70's was recorded in every month and two pairs bred within a two mile radius. Most sightings were hovering over the "Top Field" which was scythed every year by the gardeners and supported a large population of Field Mice and Short Tailed Voles but since the gardeners were made redundant in the early 70's and this area became overgrown with brambles and later allotments created, this type of habitat was lost.

One hunting over the Playing Field/Tanners Bank area on 21st November 2004 was the first I had seen in the Park for years then on 18th November 2005 I disturbed a Kestrel on the bank at the bottom of the pond which when flying laboriously away was seen to have a large young rat in its talons.

Peregrine Falcon *Falco peregrinus*
One watched flying over from the direction of the sea and hunting for a while on the "Top Field" (now allotments) which was then rough grassland on 28th November 1972. One seen overhead flying north on 27th February 2007.

Water Rail *Rallus aquaticus*
There are four records of this secretive bird, one on 11th March 1968, one wintering through January/February 1969, one on 10th January 1982 and one first seen on 31st December 2000 and present till 2nd March 2001.

Moorhen *Gallinula chloropus*
One pair present throughout 1963 after no records for a few years. Two pairs in 1968 only reared 6 young between them due to human molestation. In January 1969 11 were present but only 4 in May of the same year. Breeding was successful in 1975 with 5 young remaining till spring of 1976 when they were driven away by the resident pair. Again in 1976 they raised 4 young. There are no sightings till 1st October 2000 when one appeared and remained into 2001. A pair nested in March 2001 and 4 day old chicks were seen on 3rd June and were all fully grown on 15th July accompanied by one chick from a second brood.
　　Bred successfully in 2002 but in 2003 one pair had four

broods in April-4, May-5, July-6 and only 1 in August. Two pairs present during winter 2003/4. 3 broods were raised in 2004 by one pair. First brood of four seen on 18th May 2005. Ten present throughout autumn/winter 2005. In 2007 seven were raised and in 2008 the one pair had four broods. In 2009 the one pair had two broods with five raised and in 2010 two broods with seven altogether raised. Only one young raised in 2011.

Coot *Fulica atra*
One or two pairs were resident on the "West Pond" prior to its drainage in 1960. One tired migrant found in a nearby garden was put on the pond to recuperate in February 1976 and stayed for a week.

Lapwing *Vanellus vanellus*
Only one record of this common wader usually seen on fields and open spaces was of one which landed briefly on the frozen pond on the 9th January 2010.

Little Stint *Calidris minuta*
One arrived on 5th September 1965 and stayed for at least a week.

Dunlin *Calidris alpina*
One caught at the pond and ringed on 18th September 1966 is the only record.

Jack Snipe *Lymnocryptes minimus*
Only one record of this rare winter visitor during the winter of 1964.

Snipe *Gallinago gallinago*
Only three records of one in 1964, one in 1974 and one on 19th December 2010.

Woodcock *Scolopax rusticola*
Birds arrive from the North and Scandinavia every Autumn and occasionally appear to stay for short periods. 3 present on 25th December 1978, 1 on 15th November and 4/5 in December 2000. 1 on 19th February 2004. On 28th October 2004 I flushed 17 birds at the back of park mainly on the old railway line, this was when 100's had arrived from Scandinavia and were seen all along the coast. 2 were seen 5 days later flying through the trees disturbed by a dog. 1 seen on 5th December 2005 and 1 on 27th October 2009.

5/6 seen on 10th January 2010 and up to 6 were present from 30th November till the end of December during a period of heavy snow.

Green Sandpiper *Tringa ochropus*
Two seen flying over Park on 15th August 2006, they settled on Pond for a few minutes before flying off again.

Redshank *Tringa totanus*
Occasional birds spend a few days around the pond usually following stormy weather. The last one observed was in February 1972.

Greenshank *Tringa nebularia*
The only record of this comparatively rare wader was on 4th September 1965 when 8 flew low overhead.

Black Headed Gull *Larus ridibundus*
Herring Gull *Larus argentatus*
Great Black Backed Gull *Larus marinus*
Occasionally seen on the playing field or on the Bowling Greens, Herring Gulls regularly seen around the pond and occasionally take young Moorhen and Mallard chicks.

Stock Dove *Columba oenas*
First recorded on 21st April 2001 when 3 were seen by the pond. Nest building was observed on 22nd April and one bird was seen on the nest on 20th May. This was subsequently abandoned with Magpie predation being

suspected. 1 - 3 birds have been seen regularly throughout 2002 and 2003. On 23rd March 2004, 4 were feeding together and two nest sites were occupied at this time. On 8th March 2005 one pair were as usual at their nest site with 3 others nearby. 4 seen feeding together on 12th January 2006. Three pairs present in summer 2006 and one/two pairs have bred in the years 2007-2011. Largest count was 8 on 17th August 2009. 6 were present on 29th January 2011.

Woodpigeon *Columba palumbus*
In 1960's and 1970's 1 or 2 pairs were resident joined by 2/3 pairs for the winter months. On 22nd February 1969 25 were present for a short time. During the winter of 1971/2 5/6 were resident and during the winter of 1975/6 7 were present. In recent years suburban populations have soared and in 1999/2000 25 plus were resident, 15 pairs counted on 15th March 2001 and in December 2003 250-300 gathered at dusk and went to roost at Tanners Bank. This roost was still being used in 2010.

Collared Dove *Streptopelia decaocto*
The first pair was recorded in 1965 following a spectacular population spread northwards throughout Europe in the 1960's. In March 1967 5 were seen, 9 during 1967/8 winter and by the winter of 1972/3 a resident flock of 60 plus were present. In the 1990's numbers dwindled as Woodpigeons increased and from 2003/11 only two pairs appear to be resident.

Turtle Dove *Streptopelia turtur*
On the 12th May 1968 one was watched feeding with 5 Collared Doves in front of the Greenhouse where the gardeners put down grain each day.

Cuckoo *Cuculus canorus*
Heard occasionally in the Spring during the 1960's and 70's. One was present and seen most days between 29th June and 9th July 2007.

Barn Owl *Tyto alba*
Individual birds have been seen or heard in the past but the last one recorded during September/October 1972 was a very noisy individual.

Tawny Owl *Strix aluco*
A regular visitor. One pair was resident from 1964 to 1966.
2 were present during May 2000 and one from October
2000 was still present in January 2001. Single birds are
seen or heard almost every month by residents of Park
Avenue. One young bird was present throughout June 2006
roosting in the Pet's Cemetery. From December 2010 until
the end of 2011 two were usually found roosting in their
favourite Holly Tree or nearby Yew Tree.

Long Eared Owl *Asio otus*
Two birds were present from the 2nd November 1963 for a
week after a period of gale force winds. (Which also
brought the Scaup to the park.) One was seen in the same
area during May 2010.

Short Eared Owl *Asio flammeus*
One was seen flying over being mobbed by Crows on 30th
October 2000.

Nightjar *Caprimulgus europaeus*
Only one record of this rare nocturnal summer visitor was
of one on 17/18th May 1970.

Swift *Apus apus*
This summer visitor is present from May to August each
year, up to 20 seen feeding usually high in the sky. A late
bird was seen on 31st October 1965.

Kingfisher *Alcedo atthis*
One present from late November 1971 to March 1972
caused great local interest. It could be watched from the
side of the pond
catching and
swallowing 4
sticklebacks in 5
minutes, a sight few
people had the chance
to see previously. I
caught and ringed this
bird on the 5th January
1972. One was present
during Christmas 1999

and another celebrity was first seen on 2nd September 2000 and was still present in January 2001. Other individuals were seen on 23rd March, 3rd September and during November 2001.

One was seen regularly from 17th August till 10th November 2004. One seen on 11th September 2005 and occasionally up to the end of November.

Singles seen early July 2008, 13-30th November 2008, 10th February and 9th May 2009 and on 12th June 2010.

Wryneck *Jynx torquilla*
One seen by the old railway line on the 10th October 1963 is the only record.

Great Spotted Woodpecker *Dendrocopos major*
Five were present for a few weeks during August/ September 1968 during a large influx on the North East Coast. Following strong N.E. winds two were present for a few days from 26th September 1972, one of which was caught for ringing

Juvenile.

and proved to be of the Scandanavian race. An adult which was present from early November until late December 1972 apparently appreciated the large number of "Oak Apples" observed this year, from which it could be seen to remove the white grubs of the Gall Wasp. The year 2000 started with two seen in January, three on the 20th February and four on the 3rd March. These were very noisy individuals and could be heard all over the park drumming and calling during courtship and territorial chases. One pair nested in a tree on the site of the old North Pond and I watched food being taken into the hole in May. This is the first record of breeding in the park. Only one adult female fed the young and only one large chick could be seen at the hole towards the end of May so any other chicks below would have starved. In the following weeks after leaving the nest only one adult and one chick were seen together in confirmation of my assumptions.

An influx in December brought the numbers to four or possibly five on the 23rd with two/three seen until March 2001.

Four were present in April 2001 and a pair was seen feeding young in a nest hole in a tree by the Bowling Greens on 17th June 2001. Breeding was also confirmed in 2002, 2003 and 2004. Five seen on 6th December 2003. Two pairs present through 2004/5 winter, feeding on peanut feeders and on 16th May 2005 there were two occupied nest sites with both males

feeding the females in the nest holes. On 23rd May large young were seen looking out of both nest holes and had all left nests by 31st May.

Two pairs bred in 2006 and 2007 and three pairs in 2008. On 20th March 2009 three males and two females were seen together in one tree and two pairs were feeding young in nests on 21st May. Two pairs bred in 2010 and three pairs successfully reared young in 2011.

Skylark *Alauda arvensis*
Occasional birds were seen overhead in the 1960's and 1970's when they bred on the Golf Course.

Sand Martin *Riparia riparia*
Recorded with Swallows hawking over the pond and bowling greens each summer rarely more than half a dozen seen at once.

Swallow *Hirundo rustica*
Large numbers pass through and feed over the pond and bowling greens on spring and autumn migration. On the 2nd October 1963 a flock of over 200 passed overhead heading east. One pair successfully nested in 1964, 67 and 68 in the Potting Shed behind the Greenhouse and

attempted to nest every subsequent year only to be disturbed or robbed until 1988 when the buildings were demolished.

My first Swallow of the year 2002 was seen over the pond on 22nd April.

65 were high over the pond on 19th September 2010 then headed south.

House Martin *Delichon urbica*
As Sand Martin though much more numerous. On 13th October 1965 15 were seen, two stragglers were seen on the 16th November 1973 and one on 9th November 1975 stayed until 13th during a period of heavy rain and probably had insufficient fat reserves as a result to complete its migration. On 6th August 2001 24 hawking over the pond were chased repeatedly and unsuccessfully by a Sparrow Hawk.

On 17th May 8 were hawking over the pond.

Tree Pipit *Anthus trivialis*
One pair seen displaying during May/June 1972 presumably bred as young birds were seen later in the year.

Yellow Wagtail *Motacilla flava flavissma*
One or two were seen in the past feeding on the bowling greens but no recent records.

Grey Wagtail *Motacilla cinerea*
One on 25th March 1966, two during most of September 1972 with one still present until mid October. Two during September/ October 1974, two during October 1976 with one staying throughout the winter. Two present throughout 1977/78 winter. Single birds are now seen most months often staying for periods of a few weeks and now much more commonly seen than Pied Wagtails.

Two present during September 2009.

Pied Wagtail *Motacilla alba yarrellii*
Often seen on the bowling greens in the summer with the odd bird wintering. One here on the 30th December 2003, two on 28th April 2006 and one during May 2010.

Waxwing
Bombycilla garrulus
A single bird was seen feeding on Mountain Ash berries on 19th December 1973.

On 2nd December 2004, 8 or 9 were in the treetops and hawking for insects over the Bowling Greens.

Wren *Troglodytes troglodytes*
Probably three of four pairs resident supplemented by migrating birds. Numbers fluctuate depending on the severity of winters.

Dunnock *Prunella modularis*
An exceedingly common and successful resident.

Robin *Erithacus rubecula*
A common breeding species with numbers swelling with migration falls. In April 2001 fifteen singing males were holding territories. Four nests were found in 2011 one of which was robbed by Grey Squirrels.

Black Redstart *Phoenicurus ochruros*
One record of this uncommon passage visitor on 11th October 1981.

Redstart *Phoenicurus ochruros*
A fairly common summer visitor to Northumberland, so surprisingly only a few records of birds on passage. One seen in May 1964, two in dense fog on 4th May 1969 and three/four on the 25th September 1972. Four were present on 2nd October 1976 when hundreds were recorded on the coast throughout the county.

Whinchat *Saxicola rubetra*
Only records of this summer visitor were two grounded on

migration by bad weather on 7th May 1975 and 11 flying over going south on 22nd August 2002.

Wheatear *Oenanthe oenanthe*
A summer visitor, sometimes seen in spring or autumn passage, feeding on the bowling greens or playing field.

Blackbird *Turdus merula*
An abundant breeding resident and passage and winter visitor

A winter roost existed in the park during the 1960's and early 70's of five hundred plus when the shrubberies were regularly pruned and kept dense and therefore gave good shelter. These birds came into the park from surrounding areas at dusk and dispersed at first light. On 12th October 1997 approx 250 present, on 27th December 1999 approx 150, 200 plus in December 2000 and 300 plus in severe cold conditions on 1st January 2001. On 28th October 2004 100's were seen flying in and immediately feeding on ground when a large number of migrants were recorded all along the coast.

On 26th October approx. 150 present mainly along the old railway line in the treetops.

Fieldfare *Turdus pilaris*
Small numbers of this winter visitor are seen regularly feeding on the playing field. Tens of thousands arrive on our coast each autumn but generally continue inland to feed in open countryside. Fifty were seen flying overhead going south on 25th October 2001. Parties of 5-15 seen flying over going southwest on 28th October 2004. On the 29th December 2005, 8 seen on tree tops.

Song Thrush *Turdus philomelos*
A fairly common resident and breeding species. It has re-established itself from it's decline in the early 1960's. Five pairs recorded in March 2001 were the most seen for some years. Two pairs resident in 2009 and 2010 and two pairs raised young in 2011.

Redwing *Turdus iliacus*
This winter visitor whose numbers fluctuate according to weather conditions is present throughout most winters. In

the severe winter of 1963 hundreds were picked up dead. The largest number recorded was 400 plus roosting in December 1964. A small party of 8 present throughout January 2004. Dozens arrived on 28th October 2004 during a large influx of migrants. Early morning 17th October 2005 hundreds were present with parties of 10-20 arriving continuously while small parties moving out southerly at the same time and by mid-day only a few were to be seen. About two dozen present mid January 2010. 42 counted on 20th January 2011.

Mistle Thrush *Turdus viscivorus*
This large thrush is more often seen than heard. One/two pairs are usually resident and breed. In August 1966 approx 50 fed on three Mountain Ash trees from 22nd to 25th completely stripping the trees of berries. On 15th April 2011 the young were taken out of the nest during repeated attacks by Magpies.

Blackcap *Sylvia atricapilla*
Regularly seen in spring and autumn. One female wintered 1967/8 and was caught and ringed in January and retrapped a few weeks later still in good weight. Two wintering birds were seen on 29th February 2000. Five males were seen in May 2001 and two pairs were seen during 2003 and 2004 summers with young seen in July 2004 and a family party seen during July 2006. Five pairs were seen on 22nd May 2009. Two pairs were seen with young in July 2010 and three pairs raised young in 2011.

Garden Warbler *Sylvia borin*
Surprisingly few records. Singles seen on 4th May 1969, 14th August 2004 and 8th June 2005. Two on 30th April 2008, one on 28th May 2009 and one on 31st May 2010.

Whitethroat *Sylvia communis*
One on 21st May 2007.

Yellow-browed Warbler *Phylloscopus inornatus*
During an influx in September 2003 when a dozen birds were recorded on the Northumberland coast one was seen on the 28th.

Wood Warbler *Phylloscopus sibilatrix*
During coastal passage in August 2002 when two others were recorded on the Northumberland coast one was seen on the 25th.

Pallas's Warbler *Phylloscopus proregulus*
This rare passage vagrant from Asia is only recorded in Northumberland a few times each October/November. One was present 8/9th November 2000 during an influx when there were also two at Tynemouth and one at Whitley Bay.

Chiffchaff *Phylloscopus collybita*
As Willow Warbler but in smaller numbers. Five recorded on 16th May 1967 and a family party with newly fledged young was seen on 23rd July 200. Two seen on 23rd October 2004 when large infux of migrants on coast and one seen a few times in the same location until 14th November. Two seen 25th May 2005, three in June 2007 and two on 23rd May 2009. Two were by the bowling greens during heavy snow showers on 28th November 2010. Three pairs nested in 2011.

Willow Warbler *Phuloscopus trochilus*
Probably breeds each year. On 8th August 1965, 25 were seen. On the 4th May 1969, 20 plus were present. An adult feeding young was seen on 13th and 15th June 2005 and a pair feeding young were seen in June 2011.

Goldcrest *Regulus regulus*
This smallest British bird is regularly seen during Spring and Autumn migration sometimes in large numbers particularly after Easterly winds have carried thousands across from Scandinavia. Five recorded on 20th December 2001 and 5/6 present throughout December 2003. Four/ eight seen throughout September/October 2004 and similar number in the winter of 2005/6. A pair carrying nesting material were watched on 5th May 2006. Four on 28th November 2007, fifteen on 8th November 2008 and twelve on 9th December 2008. During 2008/9/10 seen most months.

Firecrest *Regulus igniccapillus*
A rare passage visitor, extremely rare in winter.
Only a few individuals are recorded in Northumberland
each year. A long staying individual was first seen on 13th
November 2001, again on 14th December then regularly in
the company of two Coal Tits until 19th January 2002.
Another one first seen from 20th to 23rd December 2010.

Spotted Flycatcher *Muscicapa striata*
A summer visitor, it attempted to nest in the same location
1970-72 but the eggs were stolen each year. One young
bird was caught in August 1972 but may not have been
bred locally. Two/three on 14th August 1976 and one seen
in September 2001 and one on 22nd September 2004. One
seen feeding in tree tops in south west corner by playing
field on 26th May 2005 and two on 12th September 2010.

Red Breasted Flycatcher *Ficedula parva*
Only one record of this rare passage visitor was on 1st
October 1965.

Pied Flycatcher *Ficedula hypoleuca*
This uncommon Flycatcher is only seen on migration. One
on 17th May 1967, two on 4th May 1969, three on 25th
September 1972, three males on 14th May 1975 and one
female and a young male on 11th August 2004 when there
was a large influx on the coast from Yorkshire to the
Scottish border with 60 plus on Holy Island the same day!

Long Tailed Tit *Aegithalos caudatus*
I had not recorded this species before 2000. Five were seen
on 20th February, 18 on 18th November and 23 on 16th
December 2000. On most visits during the winters of
2001/2 and 2002/2003 at least half a dozen were seen with
14 recorded on 26th November 2003 and seen throughout
December. Throughout October and November 2004, 10/15
were seen increasing to 40-50 by the end of November.
Through September/October 2005, 15/20 were present and
about 30 in December. A family party with young being fed
were seen in July 2006. 25 present all of December 2006
and 30 in January 2007. 30 in November 2008 increasing
to 50 in January 2009. In February 2009 a pair were
watched carrying feathers and at the same area with 5/6

young on 24th May. Up to 30 were seen throughout October/November and December 2010.

Blue Tit *Parus caeruleus*
Breeds each year and very common throughout the year, numbers swelling with wintering flocks. Thirty counted on 1st January 2001 and approx forty five on 30th November 2003.

Right: An illustration of a Blue Tit.

Great Tit *Parus major*
Almost as common as the Blue Tit joined by small wintering flocks. Twenty were counted on 1st January 2001 and approx twenty five on 30th November 2003.

Mike Coates

Coal Tit *Periparus ater*
Single birds are seen occasionally in wintering flocks of Blue and Great Tits. Two seen on 26th March 2000, two during December 2001 in the company of a Firecrest and three on 30th November 2003 but at least fifteen in a mixed flock with Blue and Great Tits on 7th October 2000 was exceptional. Three on 30th November 2003 and seen throughout December 2003 and throughout 2004. On 2nd June 2004 a family party with newly fledged chicks was seen proving the first record of breeding in the Park and throughout June 2005 young were being fed by adults in the same area and 3/4 seen throughout autumn. Two pairs resident in 2007/10 and probably bred each year. 3 were seen together on 17th October 2010. One pair nested in the wall near the pond in 2011.

Nuthatch *Sitta europaea*
This species who's range in England is slowly expanding northwards was first recorded in July 2002 and July 2003 when two birds had been reported.

I first saw one bird on 19th November 2003 and three were seen together on one occasion, two chasing the third individual as they are very territorial and may have been chasing a young bird out of their territory. One pair were observed carrying nesting material into a hole in a dead Elm Tree on 19th April 2004; were seen mating on the 26th and on the 18th May were feeding young in the nest. The young left the nest on 7th June and 8/9 were seen in the tree tops near the nest site roosting together on a branch. On 4th March 2005 a pair were present at the nest hole used last year and were throwing old material out of the hole but by the end of March had moved to another tree nearby and were feeding young here by 23rd May. These fledged early June and two young were seen together on 8th June being fed by both parents and four young seen with two adults in the same tree on 13th June. This tree was used again in 2006 leaving the nest early June and 7 seen on 12th. The same hole used in 2007 with four young seen in June, the pair were watched on 29th February 2008 throwing old material out of the hole and five young were seen leaving the nest in early July. The same hole was used again in 2009, 2010, 2011 and 2012 for the fifth, sixth, seventh and eighth successive years and young were fledged each year.

Treecreeper
Certhia familiaris
A breeding resident of one or two pairs, having been recorded every month of the year since 1966 although no more than four seen together. Two recorded on 12th March 2000 and three on 30th November 2003 but usually only individuals seen of this well camouflaged species. A very light

bird was seen on 22nd September 2001 and again regularly through that winter. Seven individuals seen within an hour on one day in September 2004. A pair seen carrying food into a nest in the tree next to the Nuthatches on 21st May 2009. Three single birds were seen during October and November 2010 and two together in December. Two pairs bred in 2011.

Great Grey Shrike *Lanius excubitor*
A rare passage visitor, the only one recorded in the whole of Northumberland in 2001 was one recorded being mobbed by Tits in the park on 13th January.

Jay *Garrulus gladarius*
Only one record of a bird seen briefly in an Oak tree on 29th April 2009.

Magpie *Pica pica*
Not recorded until recent years in line with its phenomenal population explosion. Two pairs were resident in the late 1990's and although breeding not confirmed now seen throughout the park the largest count being 11 around the bottom of the pond on 12th November 2003 although 33 were seen on the Golf Course in September 2002. Three were seen on 24th and 26th May 2005 at a Great Spotted Woodpecker nest hole to the consternation of the occupying pair.

Jackdaw *Corvus monedula*
Not Resident. Three birds were recorded on 2nd November
1963, two on 30th March 2004 and two on 3rd November
2005. Six accompanied about 25 Crows in one Oak tree
feeding on that year's abundant crop of acorns on 12th
October 2006. Two/three seen throughout 2008/9. Fourteen
on 28th October 2009 feeding on acorns.

Rook *Corvus frugilegus*
Occasionally birds are seen flying over to the Rookery at
Preston.

Carrion Crow *Corvus corone corone*
One or two pairs resident. It was confirmed to have bred
in 1963. Five birds regularly seen together in winter of
2003/4 and seven were feeding on acorns in one tree on
18th October 2004. Eight were calling loudly in the
treetops on 25th November 2004. On 23rd October 2005,
14 were on the bowling greens, the most recorded but then
in October 2006, during an abundant acorn crop, numbers
built up to approx 25 feeding with Magpies and Jackdaws.
On 25th April 2007 one was seen catching Mallard chicks
and 14 present on 3rd May increased to 30-40 in December
2007. Breeding confirmed in 2009 and 2010. On 2nd
November 2009, 35 were feeding on acorns and in November
2010 over 250 congregated on the tree tops at dusk.

Starling *Sturnus vulgaris*
A few pairs nest in the park and many more nest in the
surrounding streets. Large numbers gather in the tree tops
before going to communal roosts.

House Sparrow *Passer domesticus*
A common breeding resident.

Tree Sparrow *Passer montanus*
A roost of up to twenty birds used to exist in the winter
months between the pond and playing field but since the
bushes they used were cut down in 1972 they have not
been recorded.

Chaffinch *Fringilla coelebs*
Resident and are seen most months. Eight seen on the 26th

March 2000 was noted as exceptional. On the 17th June 2001 a family party of six were seen. Four seen on 7th December 2003 but in the Spring of 2006, 4/5 pairs present and in 2010, 8 often seen.

Brambling *Fringilla montifringilla*
In December 1976 a flock of about twenty were seen feeding on Beech Mast which was noticeably plentiful that winter. At least a dozen were still present in January 1977. Two pairs seen on 10th January 1982 and 18 were seen in the treetops in the Pet's Cemetery on 23rd October 2004  when there was a large influx on the coast. In October 2010, 2 were seen on the 2nd and 20 on the 9th along the old railway line. On 4th April one male was accompanying Chaffinches.

Greenfinch *Carduelis chloris*
Resident in small numbers with numbers increased in winter. The largest flock recorded was 30 plus on the 4th May 1969. It definitely bred in 1965 and I caught and ringed a female with a brood patch in 1969. Eight seen on 29th April 2000, six on 21st March and 17th June 2001. Twelve seen on 6th January 2006. Nineteen on 20th January 2007. Four on 20th April 2009.

Goldfinch *Carduelis carduelis*
This finch has increased dramatically in recent years and in the 2000's has taken over from the Greenfinch as the most common finch. It nested successfully in 1967, three young leaving a nest on 18th June and a party of five birds seen in the Autumn of that year were presumably the same birds. On 11th February 1972 three were seen, two in May 1975, one on 31st October 1976, four on 2nd March 2000

and six on 26th March 2000, seven on 21st March 2001. In January 2002, 12 were seen then on 10th March 60 plus were seen in December 2003, 40 plus seen coming into roost just before dusk. 20-30 seen in December 2005  and January 2006. 35 in December 2006, 30 on 19th January 2007 and 34 on 23rd November 2010. 14 counted on 14th March 2011.

Siskin *Carduelis spinus*
This small finch breeds in large numbers in Forestry Plantations. One female was seen feeding in treetops near the north Bowling Green on 8th April 2004 and one male in the company of eight Greenfinches on a Peanut Bird Feeder on 7th February 2006. Four by the top of the pond in a large conifer 3rd February 2008.

Linnet *Carduelis cannabina*
This bird nests on the adjacent Golf Course and parties of up to ten birds used to be seen regularly on the disused railway line which borders the east side of the park before it became so overgrown. Four were ringed in a nest on the 30th May 1965 constitute the only confirmed record of breeding in the park.

Twite *Carduelis flavirostris*
Only one record of a flock of 20/30 on 10th January 1982.

Redpoll *Carduelis cabaret*
One caught and ringed on 13th June 1969 and another on the 7th June 1972 both had brood patches suggesting they were nesting in the area. Otherwise a rather secretive bird which is rarely seen although it may be present in small numbers.

Crossbill *Loxia curvirostra*
In February 1963 a pair were watched for some time on the "Top Field" feeding in thistle heads.

Bullfinch *Pyrrhula pyrrhula*

On 27th May 2005 I saw a pair by the "Daisy Field" which was the only record in almost 50 years of birdwatching in the Park. One male was seen on a few occasions in the next few weeks, suggesting possible nesting but then no other sightings. In July 2008 a family party with at least three young were seen. On 20th December 2010 a male was seen flying over the pond and then one was heard calling two days later in the same area. In 2011 there was only one sighting of a male on 17th February.

Snow Bunting *Plectrophenax nivalis*
There is only one record of this rare winter visitor, when on the 13th October 1963 one was seen by the pond.

List of Bird Species recorded
1960 – 2011

113 Species of Birds recorded 1960-2011
Of which 36 are known to have bred in the park *

Mute Swan *
Whooper Swan
Grey Lag Goose
Mandarin
Wigeon
Teal
Mallard *
Pintail
Shoveler
Pochard
Tufted Duck *
Scaup
Goosander
Red Legged Partridge
Grey Partridge
Pheasant
Little Grebe
Cormorant
Little Egret
Grey Heron
Sparrow Hawk *
Buzzard
Kestrel
Peregrine Falcon
Water Rail
Moorhen *
Coot
Lapwing
Little Stint
Dunlin
Jack Snipe
Snipe
Woodcock
Green Sandpiper
Redshank
Greenshank
Black Headed Gull

Herring Gull
Great Black Backed Gull
Stock Dove *
Wood Pigeon *
Collared Dove *
Turtle Dove
Cuckoo
Barn Owl
Tawny Owl
Long Eared Owl
Short Eared Owl
Nightjar
Swift
Kingfisher
Wryneck
Great Spotted Woodpecker*
Skylark
Sand Martin
Swallow *
House Martin
Tree Pipit
Yellow Wagtail
Grey Wagtail
Pied Wagtail *
Waxwing
Wren *
Dunnock *
Robin *
Black Redstart
Redstart
Whinchat
Wheatear
Blackbird *
Fieldfare
Song Thrush *
Redwing
Mistle Thrush *
Blackcap *

Garden Warbler
Whitethroat
Yellow-browed Warbler
Wood Warbler
Pallas's Warbler
Chiffchaff *
Willow Warbler *
Goldcrest *
Firecrest
Spotted Flycatcher
Red Breasted Flycatcher
Pied Flycatcher
Long Tailed Tit *
Blue Tit *
Great Tit *
Coal Tit *
Nuthatch *
Treecreeper *
Great Grey Shrike
Jay
Magpie *
Jackdaw
Rook
Carrion Crow *
Starling *
House Sparrow *
Tree Sparrow
Chaffinch *
Brambling
Greenfinch *
Goldfinch *
Siskin
Linnet *
Twite
Redpoll
Crossbill
Bullfinch *
Snow Bunting

Totals of Birds ringed in Park

1963–1979   2,074 BIRDS OF 38 SPECIES

SPECIES	ADULT	NESTLING
MALLARD	2	
SCAUP	1	
MOORHEN	5	
DUNLIN	1	
COLLARED DOVE	1	2
TAWNY OWL	1	
KINGFISHER	1	
GT SPOTTED WOODPECKER	1	
SWIFT	39	
SWALLOW	6	6
CARRION CROW	0	1
GREAT TIT	27	
BLUE TIT	210	2
COAL TIT	1	
WREN	15	
MISTLE THRUSH	1	3
FIELDFARE	2	
SONG THRUSH	104	2
REDWING	134	
BLACKBIRD	945	11
REDSTART	1	
ROBIN	84	
BLACKCAP	4	
WILOW WARBLER	4	
CHIFFCHAFF	2	
GOLDCREST	2	
SPOTTED FLYCATCHER	3	
GREY WAGTAIL	1	
DUNNOCK	84	
STARLING	125	10
GREENFINCH	43	6
GOLDFINCH	0	3
LINNET	2	4
REDPOLL	16	
CHAFFINCH	13	
BRAMBLING	1	
HOUSE SPARROW	140	
TREE SPARROW	2	
TOTAL	2,024	50

Birds ringed elsewhere and retrapped in the Park

Ring Number	Species	Age	Date	Comments
SC39982	Swift	AD	29.05.65	Holywell Ponds
			29.06.67	Northumberland Park
HB80695	Blue Tit	1Y	28.08.66	Sheepwash, Ashington
		AD	17.12.67	Northumberland Park
CA75896	Blackbird	1YF	20.10.65	Priors Park, Tynemouth
		ADF	19.11.67	Northumberland Park
		ADF	07.12.68	Northumberland Park
		ADF	28.06.70	Found dead-Tynemouth 6 years old
CS40586	Blackbird	JUV	22.09.67	Priors Park, Tynemouth
		1YF	27.01.68	Northumberland Park
		ADF	25.01.69	Northumberland Park
CJ47951	Blackbird	ADF	18.04.74	Fair Isle, Shetland
		ADF	19.10.74	Northumberland Park
HC36188	Chaffinch	1YM	28.10.66	Hartley, Whitley Bay
		1YM	28.12.66	Northumberland Park
BJ12356	Greenfinch	ADM	14.02.70	Priors Park, Tynemouth
		ADM	13.12.70	Northumberland Park

Pullus   Young ringed in the nest

1Y   Bird in its first year

FG   Full grown not necessarily adult

AD   Adult

F or M   denotes female or male if the sex can be determined

Recoveries of Birds ringed in the Park

(REPORTED BY THE GENERAL PUBLIC)

Ring Number	Species	Age	Date	Comments
SS54933	Moorhen	AD	08.02.69 11.06.77	Northumberland Park Found dying, at least 9 years old
SS54934	Moorhen	1Y	08.02.69 16.07.70	Born in Park – Summer 1968 Wallsend – Shot
SE35556	Swift	AD	24.06.67 16.05.68	Northumberland Park Holywell – retrapped
SE35597	Swift	AD	29.06.67 30.05.68	Northumberland Park Whitley Bay – found dead
HR12060	Swallow	Pullus AD	06.08.68 01.07.69	Hatched in Potting Shed Stocksfield – nesting on Farm
CA22564	Blackbird	1YM	14.02.63 10.04.66	Northumberland Park Vastalanda, Sweden
CA22593	Blackbird	FG	21.12.63 17.04.64	Northumberland Park Aalborg, Jutland, Denmark
CV86040	Blackbird	1YM	24.12.66 00.06.71	Northumberland Park Westerwanne, Germany – Killed by cat
CS40594	Blackbird	1YF	21.10.67 10.10.68	Northumberland Park Monkseaton – found dead
CS70514	Blackbird	ADM	24.11.68 02.12.71	Northumberland Park Hartlepool
CR44735	Blackbird	1YM	24.11.68 20.09.69	Northumberland Park Tosse, Alysborg, Sweden

CP20759	Blackbird	ADF	20.02.70 00.06.71	Northumberland Park Voore, Rakvere, Estonia – Found injured
CP20784	Blackbird	1YF	20.10.70 16.03.77	Northumberland Park Crawcrook – found dead
CJ45457	Blackbird	1YM	14.10.72 26.02.73	Northumberland Park Fullwell – found dead
CN87976	Blackbird	1YF	19.01.72 Unknown	Northumberland Park Zwin Knokke-Sur- Mere, Belgium
CJ92894	Blackbird	FGM	17.03.73 00.09.74	Northumberland Park Akerhus, Oslo, Norway Found dead
CB51564	Redwing	FG	28.12.64 21.04.70	Northumberland Park Skegness – found dead
CS70541	Redwing	1Y	29.12.68 21.02.69	Northumberland Park Seaton Sluice – found dead
CP55251	Redwing	1Y	04.01.70 23.02.70	Northumberland Park Tynemouth – found dead
CN60405	Song Thrush	AD	22.01.72 02.06.77	Northumberland Park Murton, North Shields – found dead
JK18295	Blue Tit	1Y	28.10.72 18.08.73	Northumberland Park Medburn, Ponteland
CR83735	Starling	ADM	16.02.69 29.05.70	Northumberland Park Melkoniemi, Parikkla, Finland – found dead
XX76756	Starling	ADF	27.12.76 08.04.78	Northumberland Park Holywell Dene – killed by cat

These records clearly illustrate the fact that the majority of
Blackbirds that spend the winter with us return to Scandinavia
and Eastern Europe to nest in the summer months.

Some of the most notable retrapped Birds in the Park

Ring Number	Species	Age	Date	Comments
AN23288	Great Tit	ADF	28.12.64	Winters only
		ADF	14.01.68	
		ADF	30.12.69	Five years old
HB76875	Blue Tit	1Y	11.12.65	Winters only
		AD	11.12.67	
		AD	28.01.68	
		AD	06.10.68	
PJ0161	Wren	AD	03.01.71	4 consecutive winters
		AD	06.12.71	
		AD	26.11.72	
		AD	31.12.73	
CS70601	Song Thrush	JUV	27.07.68	Summer only
		AD	24.08.69	
CR83758	Redwing	1Y	12.02.69	
		AD	20.04.70	Found dead
CV65938	Blackbird	1YM	19.10.66	
		1YM	08.01.67	
		1YM	08.03.67	
		ADM	18.04.69	
		ADM	30.12.69	
CS40742	Blackbird	ADM	02.12.67	Adult in 1967
		ADM	07.12.68	therefore at least
		ADM	14.10.72	6 years old in 1972
CS70221	Blackbird	1YM	17.12.67	
		ADM	01.12.68	
		ADM	10.10.69	
		ADM	08.11.73	Found dead in Tynemouth 6 years old
CS70272	Blackbird	1YM	30.12.67	
		ADM	27.07.69	No apparent migration as present in summer and winter
		ADM	08.07.70	
		ADM	22.01.72	

HB76857	Robin	FG	28.11.65	Winters only
		AD	26.12.66	NB Not possible to
		AD	07.12.68	tell the sex of Robins.
HR12098	Dunnock	1Y	08.12.68	
		AD	13.12.70	
		AD	10.06.74	Found dead – 6 years old

It will be noted that many birds caught and later retrapped in the winter months are not present in the summer months and vica versa; illustrating the migration south in the winter of our breeding birds and their places being taken by Northern and Scandinavian birds.

BIRD RINGING – WHY?

Bird ringing is a useful research tool for the study of migratory birds and their conservation. It allows birds to be individually marked and their movements and other life history traits to be tracked over time. Through ringing, information on dispersal, migration, longevity, behaviour, survival rate, reproductive success and population trends of migratory birds can be obtained.

Bird Ringing entails catching birds and placing a small, unique numbered, weightless ring on the bird's leg. The ring has absolutely no effect on the bird's ability to fly, feed and breed as has been proved by long term tests. Details such as age, sex, weight and wing measurements are taken quickly and carefully. The bird is then released. Each person involved in the ringing of birds has to go through a rigorous training programme with highly experienced ringers before becoming licensed by the British Trust for Ornithology to ring birds on their own. It is illegal to catch wild birds without a ringing licence.

Whenever ringed birds are found dead, or re-trapped they can be identified and their movements can be tracked.

Mammals recorded in the Park

Most visitors to the park will be aware of the various bird species but are unlikely and would probably not expect to see any "wild animals" as birds are more easily observed whereas most animals (apart from domestic ones) are nocturnal and secretive by nature.

The only resident animal likely to be seen is the **Rabbit** *Oryctolagus cuniculus* whose numbers fluctuate dramatically between regular outbreaks of myxomatosis. Since the resident gardeners left their numbers have increased due to the increase in uncultivated areas. In Spring 2004 up to ten regularly seen and by June with young emerging up to twenty seen.

Hedgehogs *Erinaceus europaeus*
Used to be numerous – I remember in the 1960's and 70's regularly seeing one or more in late summer evenings. One dead young one seen in late 2003 suggested breeding in the Park and one dead adult was seen on Tynemouth Road 26th April 2004. I saw fresh tracks in soft mud in August 2004 of apparently one adult.

Fox *Vulpes vulpes*
In common with a national trend the fox is becoming more of a town than country dweller (well you don't see many Fox Hunts in North Shields) and is regularly heard barking in the night by residents of Park Avenue and Park Terrace. I almost bumped into one at 5am one summer morning in 2003 which stared at me in unbelief before turning and disappearing in a flash. They are known to travel along the old railway line from the direction of Priors Park where they have raised cubs and in the summer of 2004 I watched one on several occasions at their earths down Tanners Bank. By 2009 although mainly seen by the early morning dog walkers, they are regularly seen at all hours even seen walking down the main drive at midday.

Badger *Meles meles*
Surprisingly evidence of this shy nocturnal animal was recorded by the Northumberland Badger Group along the old railway line when the Link Path was being constructed in June 2010. It was believed that it/they were only using the wildlife corridor and were not resident. Then in May 2011 an adult was found dead in Mariner's Lane Allotments, only yards away from this area.

Roe Deer *Capreolus capreolus*
You might think that this deer averaging 70 cms at the shoulder could not remain hidden in the Park yet single deer have been recorded, one apparently staying for a few days or more in 2002 and seen by a few people and I found some tracks at this time. Individuals have been seen crossing the Golf Course and seen down Tanners Bank and once on Tynemouth Pier suggesting use of this wildlife corridor possibly from Holywell Dene and beyond where Deer are resident.

One had been killed by a car in 2006 crossing the road from the Golf Course. One was present during the night of 17th January 2011.

Grey Squirrel
Sciurus carolinensis
This omnivorous squirrel whose range is ever increasing was seen by me as the first record for the Park on 12th September 2006. There was an abundant crop of Beech Nuts and Acorns this year which may well be the attraction. Although only one was seen, there could easily be others present, hidden while the trees are still in full leaf. Another individual (or the same one?) was seen in the same area early July 2009 and then 14th July 2010 two were seen together at the end of July 2010 and throughout the autumn three were seen most days feeding on Beech Mast, Acorns and Conkers.

Two smaller squirrels seen in 2011 appeared to be young.

Of the smaller mammals the **Brown Rat** *Rattus rattus* is probably resident though rarely seen except when numbers explode, then often seen particularly scavenging around the pond. When the gardeners fed the ducks daily it was regularly seen round the pond and swimming to the island. In the winter of 2005/6 a family were regularly seen feeding on peanuts, becoming quite tame as this young one photographed from 3 feet away shows.

The population status of the smaller mammals is difficult to determine.

The **House Mouse** *Mus musculus* and the slightly larger and more colourful **Wood Mouse** *Apodemus sylvaticus* are present, proved by specimens I have caught in live traps and dead ones seen on occasions, probably killed and left by cats.

The **Short-tailed Vole** *Microtus agrestis* differing from Mice by having a thick blunt head and inconspicuous ears used to be common on the rough grass of the "Top Field" before the allotments were there and before the banks became overgrown with brambles and scrub.

Of the native shrews, identified by their size, being almost half that of mice and having a very pointed muzzle and a relatively short tail the **Common Shrew** *Sorex araneus* and the **Pygmy Shrew** *Sorex minutes* have occasionally been found dead and even more rarely seen.

Common Pipistrelle Bat *Pipistrellus pipistrellus* is Britain's smallest and most common species and is regularly seen on summer evenings. Wingspan being 190-250 mm and head and body length 35-45mm. Their flight is fast and jerky as they pursue small insects which a single Pipistrelle may consume up to 3,000 in a night eaten in flight. Buildings are the most favoured roost sites, typically on the outside under soffits or behind hanging wall tiles. They rarely enter roof spaces. At least 6 were watched on 29th September 2011.

Nathusius Pipistrelle Bat *Pipistrellus nathusil* is larger than the Common Pipistrelle and is a rare recent arrival from the continent and has a recognisably different echolocation call. One was identified by its call during a survey in August 2009 and one was watched for 15 minutes flying around the pond mid-day on 13th January 2011.

Natterer's Bat *Myotis nattereri*
A medium sized bat which uses tunnels and caves in which to hibernate. On 18th August 2006 at 5pm I was surprised to see an individual flying up and down the pond

for a few minutes in bright sunshine taking 3 or 4 drinks as it flew. It then disappeared into the tall oaks. Three days later on the 21st at 12.30 mid-day I witnessed the same occurrence, it was a very warm day and presumably the bat was thirsty.

Whiskered Bat *Myotis mystaginus*
Brandts Bat *Myotis brandtii*
Whiskered and Brandts were only separated as different species in the 1970's and are only marginally bigger than a Pipistrelle, have broader wings and fly much slower and in a less fluttery fashion. One of these two species was identified by its call during a survey in August 2009 but as both species sound identical cannot be positively identified unless physically examined.

I have on a few occasions seen larger bats in the Park that could be either, or both of:

Noctule Bat *Nyctalus noctula* is one of the largest British species and usually the first to appear in the evening and is a relatively common species. Noctules are particularly attracted to street lamps to feed on moths and are primarily tree dwellers and live mainly in rot holes and woodpecker holes. Wingspan is 320-400mm and head and body length 60-82 mm.

Brown Long Eared Bat *Plecotus auritus* are medium sized bats with ears almost as long as their bodies, although not always obvious; head and body length 37-48 mm and wingspan 230-285mm. They are the second most common species in Britain found throughout the UK. Long Eared Bats roost in particularly large old roof spaces on the roof timbers of the apex particularly by the ridge ends and chimneys.

Amphibians recorded in the Park

Common Frog *Rana temporaria temporaria*
They are not generally seen in the Park except in March/
April when fluctuating numbers (20-60 seen in different
years) return to the pond to spawn.

Smooth or Common Newt *Triturus vulgaris vulgaris*
One day in the early 1970's I was surprised to find a single
specimen in the small stream that runs below the
allotments on the west of the pond. About fifteen were
released in the Iris bed at the top of the pond in May 2009
after the pond where they came from was filled in.

Red Eared Slider Terrapin *Trachemys scripta elegans*
Two of these popular pets, originally from the southern
states of America, have been observed in the pond for at
least four years as at summer 2012. Approximately nine
inches in length, they presumably having outgrown their
tanks have been "released" by their owner.

Dragonflies recorded in the Park

Dragonflies are seen most summer months, usually hawking around the pond or in the vicinity – the following were identified by me between 2004 and 2010.

Emperor Dragonfly *Anax imperator* Two seen hawking Sept 2004

Common Darter *Sympetrum striolatum* One seen on 28th August 2006. 16 on 31st August and 5 on 8th September 2006. 2 on 28th July 2007. 2 on 23rd July 2009.

Ruddy Darter *Sympetrum sanguineum* up to a dozen September 2004 around pond and seen in previous years but none seen in 2005. 2 on 8th October 2008.

Migrant Hawker *Aeshna mixta* One seen 19th July 2005, 14th August 2007, 13th and 20th October 2008 all by the site of the greenhouses.

Southern Hawker *Aeshna cyanea* One seen 8th September 2005 by greenhouse site and one in the same area on 7th and 28th August 2006. Two on 31st August 2006 and one on 6th August 2007.

Brown Hawker *Aeshna grandis* One was seen over the pond on 3rd November 2006.

Common Hawker *Aeshna juncea* One seen by greenhouse site on 3rd August 2009.

Common Hawker.

Butterflies recorded in the Park

There are 59 recognised resident species of butterflies in Britain compared with over 2,000 species of moths.

No previous survey appears to have been done in the park however The Butterfly Conservation Group have records for the area NZ 3668 which includes the southern border of the Park and then down Tanners Bank to the riverside. Here they have recorded fifteen species all designated "common" – Large and Small Skippers; Large, Small and Green Winged Whites; Orange Tip; Small Copper; Common Blue; Peacock; Painted Lady; Comma; Red Admiral; Small Tortoiseshell; Meadow Brown and Wall Brown.

I have now recorded all of these species (and more) in Northumberland Park.

I only started to record butterflies in the park in the summer of 2004 and the summer was particularly wet and so the sunny days when I could look for butterflies in flight were very limited. 2005 was better and July 2006 produced a heatwave, 2007 and 2008 had torrential rain during much of July and August and again 2009 and 2010 were very poor summers. A promising start to 2011 saw the return of Holy Blues but the rest of the summer was again disappointing.

Up to 2012 I have recorded the following **21 species**:

Large Skipper
Ochlodes sylvanus
Although called the Large Skipper, the Skippers are our smallest butterflies being less than 1inch/ 3cms across the wings. They favour rough grassland on which they lay their eggs. There is a colony along the old railway line and up to 25 were seen here in July 2011.

Small Skipper
Thmelicus sylvestris
Like the Large Skippers there is a colony and between 10 and 20 are seen in June and July near Tynemouth Metro line.

Large White
Pieris Brassicae
A common and conspicuous Butterfly often flying amongst the treetops. It over winters as a pupa and our native population is increased by continental migrants. Earliest I have noted was one on 20th March 2009 and the latest was one on the 6th September 2011. On warm sunny summer days one or two dozen may be seen. Highest count in 2011 was 14 on 15th August.

Small White
Pieris Rapae
Almost as common as the Large White and also over winters as a pupa. A late record was one on a very warm and sunny 27th October 2005. Earliest record is two on 5th April 2011. 12 seen on 12th August 2010 is the highest count.

Green Veined White
Pieris Napi
Often mistaken for Small White but the veins on the wings are conspicuous when at rest. It over winters as a pupa. Rarely more than one or two seen. Two seen on 30th April then one on 2nd July were the only records in 2011.

Orange Tip
Anthocharis cardamines
A relatively common increasing species but few seen in the Park. The female lacks the orange wing tips and can be mistaken for a Small White if the beautifully

marked undersides of the hind wings are not seen.

Purple Hairstreak
Neozephyrus quercus
This small rare butterfly lives in colonies on the tops of Oak Trees and is consequently difficult to observe. The only records are two

seen on 26th August 2010 and a single specimen nearby a few days later but there could be a lot more in the treetops!

White Letter Hairstreak
Satyrium w-album
A rare butterfly that is extending its range northwards but not previously recorded north of Durham. One was seen feeding on Lime Tree flowers on 1st and 5th August 2006 along with 3/4

Holly Blues caused great interest. Two seen on 31st July 2007 in same area.

Small Copper
Lycaena phlaeas
This delightful little butterfly, only an inch from wingtip to wingtip occurs in small self-contained colonies. Three were seen along the old railway line in August 2010 and one in the same area in August 2011.

Camberwell Beauty
Nymphalis antiopa
A rare migrant from Scandinavia rarely seen in Britain. One was seen on 14th and 15th August 2006 on the ground near the Correction House in a weak condition found by Paul Beagerie.

Peacock
Inachis Io
A large most attractive hibernating butterfly, the larva of which feeds on nettles. It lays dense clusters of up to 500 eggs on the underside of nettle leaves in May/June. Adults can live for up to 10 months and can therefore be seen most months. Singles seen regularly and occasionally two or three seen.

Comma
Polygonia c-album
The unusual shaped wings and almost orange colour make this quite unmistakable. It has extended its range in recent years; the larva feeds on nettles and the adult hibernates. It can be seen most months

of the year. One was seen in late November 2007 and an unusual early record of seven seen on 18th March 2009.

Meadow Brown
Maniola Jurtina
A very common butterfly in grassy fields and hedgerows which over winters as a larva. Singles often seen around the grass banks by the pond. Ten seen on the old railway line and eight around the Park in July 2006 was an unusually large count.

Speckled Wood
Pararge aegeria

A few individuals were first seen in the park in July 2006 following a national trend of northern expansion of its range. Then a spectacular increase in numbers in July/ August 2007 and

then 10 seen along length of Park in October and then a very late record of one on a sunny 11th November. By 2010/2011 well established and often the commonest butterfly seen in the park with 20 seen many days and the highest count one day of 28.

Wall Brown
Lasiommata megera

This butterfly recolonized Northumberland in the late 1970's after disappearing at the end of the 19th century. It over winters as a larva having fed on various grasses. Loves hot sunny places and often basks on the ground. Has two broods usually in April/June and July/September. Only a few records in the park in 2005 and 2010.

Ringlet
Aphantopus hyperantus

This butterfly which is easily mistaken for a Meadow Brown is only in flight from June to August. It has only been seen along the old railway line in 2010 and 2011.

Holly Blue
Celastrina Argiolus
A rare highflying butterfly has extended its range northwards in recent years. It feeds on Holly and lays its eggs in the buds of Ivy. The first one recorded in the park was in August 2004 then three or four seen each summer up till June 2008 then following wet summers not seen in 2009 or 2010 following a regional trend. The park was "re-colonised" in 2011 with high flying butterflies seen. First one on April then up to six by July.

Common Blue
Polyommatus Icarus
The most common small blue butterfly of flowery grasslands favouring Trefoil and Clover flowers. Three were seen in July 2006 on the old railway line near Mariner's Lane and two in the same location in August 2010.

Red Admiral
Vanessa atalanta
The most recognisable and familiar migratory butterfly with large numbers arriving from Southern Europe and North Africa in May/June returning south in late summer. Some do overwinter here and it can be seen most months.
Large numbers can be seen feeding on flowering shrubs and up to twenty five are often seen in September on the Strawberry Tree.

Painted Lady
Vanessa cardui
This long distance migrant spreads northwards from North Africa into Europe and Britain each year and does not appear to be able to survive our winters. Usually only

singles seen but three were recorded in June 2009 after millions arrived in Britain, after an amazing 1,000 mile migration from North Africa on what could be the largest influx in decades. Eight seen on the railway line in August were bright second generation from eggs laid by the migrants in June.

Small Tortoiseshell
Aglaise urticae
One of the most common resident British butterflies and one of the first to emerge after hibernation, its caterpillars feed on nettles yet not common in the park. Not recorded every year and

often only singles seen. Eight in July 2010 being the maximum ever seen.

Flora/Trees recorded in the Park

Many ornamental and unusual trees and shrubs were planted in the park in its early days which are now large mature specimens and many being only single examples. As a result in this small park I have identified **65 different tree and 32 different shrub species**.

This view from overhead looking east shows how dense the tree canopy has become as the majority of the trees planted when the park was created have matured.

The park is registered as being located on a Local Wildlife Corridor adjacent to the River Tyne Strategic Wildlife Corridor as identified in the Tyne and Wear Nature Conservation Strategy 1988.

Although some areas have been planted with ornamental species much of the park is characterised by native broadleaved trees and some areas devoid of a scrub layer and not covered by the rapidly spreading Brambles (which were kept localised as these areas were scythed in the winter months when the gardeners were employed in the Park) have retained a remnant woodland groundflora.

The wooded areas are dominated by Sycamore (Acer pseudoplantanus), Wych Elm (Ulmus grabla), Ash

(Fraxinus excelsior) and Beech (Fagus sylvatica). In May 2004 I counted over **1,400 trees**, of which over 850 were Sycamore representing 58% of the total. Wych Elm was the second most common although the majority of the 156 counted representing 11% were saplings. Third most common was Ash with 91 representing 6%, a quarter of which are in the dene by the Bowling Greens. Fourth was Holly where 64 represented 4% of the total and, Beech being the fifth with 56 representing almost 4% although like the Elms the majority were saplings under 6 feet which is encouraging as the majority of the Sycamores are reaching the end of their lives which will obviously leave large areas devoid of trees.

Along the fence in Park Terrace in the allotment area there has been planted a screen of 70 Copper Beech trees. At this date there are still standing about 30 large dead Elms (not included in my figures), the majority of which were the largest trees in the park and were killed by Dutch Elm Disease. These rotting trees are however ideal for the Great Spotted Woodpeckers and Nuthatches and have resulted in their successful nesting which had not occurred in the park previously. During the night of 7th January 2005 when winds of 70 miles per hour were recorded, 8 of these large dead trees were blown down and presumably the remainder will have to be felled at some time to prevent the spread of this disease.

Of the 65 species of trees are some unusual species of which I have only found single specimens, among these are Sessile Oak, Holm Oak, Contorted Willow, Turkish Hazel, Strawberry Tree, Sweet Chestnut and the Service Tree of Fontainebleau.

The main shrubberies were planted in strips behind the original flower beds and run

Sessile Oak.

124

parallel to the main paths. These mainly comprise of evergreens such as Laurel, Privet, Daisy Bush and Senecio. When the gardeners were still employed in the park these were regularly pruned and in the case of

Strawberry Tree.

some Privets and Boxes were clipped in various shapes and the larger evergreens being kept dense provided valuable secure nesting sites and winter roosting for the numerous winter visitors principally Blackbirds and Redwings. Since the gardeners left the Park the bushes have grown unchecked and have become "leggy" and indeed in the case of the majority of the Laurels reached over 20 feet tall and no longer provide suitable nesting or roosting sites.

Many areas devoid of a scrub layer have a secondary woodland ground flora including remnant patches of old woodland species (some of which have been planted). Typical species include Cow Parsley (Anthriscus sylvestris), Hogweed (Heracleum sphondylium), Hedge Mustard (Sisymbrium officinale), Nipplewort (Lapsana communis), Ivy Leaved Speedwell (Veronica hederifolia), Foxglove (Digitalis purpurea), Red Campion (Silene dioica), Broad Buckler Fern (Dryopteris dilitata), Male Fern (Dryopteris filix-mas), Wild Garlic (Allium ursinum), Lesser Celandine (Ranunculus ficaria) and Giant Bellflower (Campanula latifolia). A number of ornamental bulbs have also been introduced into these areas including Daffodil (Narcissus spp), Spanish Bluebell (Hyacinthoides hispanicus) and Snowdrop (Galanthus nivalis).

TREES

* Single Specimen

Abies grandis	Grand Fir
Acer platanoides	Norway Maple
Acer pseudoplatanus	Sycamore
Aesculus x carnea	Red Horse Chestnut
Aesculus hippocastanum	Horse Chestnut
Alnus glutinosa	Common Alder
Arbutus unedo *	Strawberry Tree
Betula pendula	Silver Birch
Betula pubescens	Downy Birch
Castanea sativa *	Sweet Chestnut
Chamaecyparis lawsoniana	Lawson Cypress
Chamaecyparis pisifera *	Sawara Cypress
Corylus avellana	Common Hazel
Corylus colurna *	Turkish Hazel
Cotoneaster frigidus	Himalayan Tree-Cotoneaster
Crataegus monogyna	Hawthorn
Cupressocyparis leylandii	Leyland Cypress
Cupressus macrocarpa	Monterey Cypress
Eucalyptus niphopila	Snow Gum
Fagus sylvatica	Beech
Fagus sylvatica purpurea	Copper Beech
Fraxinus excelsior	Ash
Fraxinus excelsior pendula *	Weeping Ash
Fraxinus americana *	White Ash
Ilex alterclarensis	Highclere Holly
Ilex aquifolium	Holly
Juniperus communis	Juniper
Juniperus chinensis *	Chinese Juniper
Laburnum anagyroides	Laburnum
Malus sylvestris	Apple
Malus floribunda	Japanese Crab Apple
Nothofagus antarctica	Antarctic Beech
Picea abies	Norway Spruce
Pinus nigra	Corsican Pine
Pinus sylvestris	Scots Pine
Populus canescans	Grey Poplar
Populus nigra *	Lombardy Poplar
Populus trichocarpa *	Western Balsam Poplar
Prunus avium	Wild Cherry
Prunus cerasifera	Cherry Plum
Prunus dulcis	Almond
Prunus laurocerasus	Cherry Laurel
Prunus pissardii	Myrobalan Plum
Prunus serrulata	Japanese Cherry
Quercus cerris	Turkey Oak
Quercus ilex *	Holm Oak
Quercus petraea *	Sessile Oak
Quercus robur	English Oak
Quercus rubra	Red Oak
Salix caprea	Goat Willow
Salix fragilis	Crack Willow

Salix matsudana *	Contorted Willow
Sorbus aria	Whitebeam
Sorbus aucuparia	Rowan (Mountain Ash)
Sorbus intermedia *	Swedish Whitebeam
Sorbus latifolia *	Service Tree of Fontainebleau
Sorbus torminalis *	Wild Service Tree
Taxus baccata	Common Yew
Taxus baccata fastigiata	Irish Yew
Thuja plicata *	Western Red Cedar
Tilia cordata	Small-leafed Lime
Tilia euchlora *	Caucasian Lime
Tilia europaea	Common Lime
Ulmus carpinifolia	Smooth-leaved Elm
Ulmus glabra	Wych Elm

SHRUBS

Aronia melanocarpa	Black Chokeberry
Aucuba japonica variegata	Laurel
Aucuba japonica	Spotted Laurel
Berberis stenophylla	Barberry
Buddleia davidii	Butterfly Bush
Buxus sempervirens	Box
Cornus sanguinea	Common Dogwood
Cotoneaster sp.	Cotoneaster
Crataegus monogyna	Hawthorn
Euonymus japonica spp.	Euonymus
Fatsia japonica	Caster Oil Plant
Forsythia intermedia spectabilis	Golden Bells
Hebes various spp.	Veronica
Hypericum hidcote	St John's Wort
Ilex spp.	Hybrid Holly
Ligustrum ovalifolium aureum	Golden privet
Ligustrum vulgare	Privet
Mahonia japonica	Mahonia
Olearia macrodonta	Daisy Bush (Holly)
Olearia haastii	Daisy Bush
Prunus laurocerasus	Cherry Laurel
Rhododendron spp.	Rhododendron
Ribes sanguineum	Flowering Currant
Salix viminalis	Common Osier
Sambuscus laciniata	Parsley-leaved Elder
Sambuscus nigra	Elder
Senecio greyi	Senecio
Skimmia japonica	Skimmia
Symphoricarpos rivularis	Snowberry
Syringa vulgaris	Lilac
Ulex europaeus	Gorse
Viburnum rhytidophyllum	Viburnum

LIVERWORTS

Lunuloria cruciata	Liverwort
Pellia epiphylla	Liverwort

MOSSES

Eurhynchium praelongum
Fissidens taxifolius
Mnium hornum

FERNS AND HORSETAILS

Dryopteris dilitata	Broad Buckler Fern
Dryopteris filix-mas	Male Fern

DICOTS

Aegopodium podagraria	Ground Elder, Goutweed, Bishopweed
Alliaria petiolata	Garlic Mustard
Anemone nemorosa	Wood Anemone
Anthriscus sylvestris	Cow Parsley
Bellis perennis	Daisy
Calystegia sepium	Great Bindweed
Campanula latifolia	Giant Bellflower, Throatwort
Capsella bursa-pastoris	Shepherd's Purse
Cardamine pratensis	Lady's Smock, Cuckoo Flower, Milk-maids
Centaurea nigra	Hardhead
Centaurea scabiosa	Common Knapweed
Chrysanthemum leucanthemum	Ox-Eye Daisy
Chrysanthemum parthenium	Feverfew
Cerastium vulgatum	Mouse Eared Chickweed
Cirsium arvense	Creeping Thistle
Cirsium vulgare	Spear Thistle
Conopodium majus	Pignut
Convolvulus arvensis	Field Bindweed
Crepis capillaris	Smooth Hawksbeard
Digitalis purpurea	Foxglove
Epilobium angustifolium	Rosebay Willow-herb, Fireweed
Epilobium montanum	Broad-leaved Willow-herb
Galeopsis tetrahit	Common Hemp Nettle
Galium aparine	Goosegrass, Cleavers
Geranium robertianum	Herb Robert
Geum urbanum	Herb Bennet, Wood Avens
Hedera helix	Ivy
Heracleum sphondylium	Hogweed, Cow Parsnip
Hypericum androsaemum	Tutsan
Hypericum perforatum	Common St John's Wort
Lamium album	White Dead Nettle
Lamium purpureum	Red Dead Nettle
Lathyrus aphaca	Meadow Pea
Lapsana communis	Nipplewort
Leontodon hispidus	Greater Hawkbit
Lotus corniculatu	Bird's foot Trefoil
Linaria vulgaris	Common Toadflax
Lunaria annua	Honesty
Melandrium dioicum	Red Campion
Myosotis sylvatica	Wood Forget Me Not
Onopordum acanthium	Scotch Thistle
Plantago lanceolata	Ribwort Plantain

Plantago major	Ratstail Plantain
Plantago media	Hoary Plantain
Potentilla reptans	Creeping Cinquefoil
Polygonatum multiflorum	Common Solomon's Seal
Primula veris	Cowslip
Primula vulgaris	Primrose
Ranunculus acris	Meadow Buttercup
Ranunculas auricomus	Wood Goldilocks
Ranunculus bulbosus	Bulbous Buttercup
Ranunculus ficaria	Lesser Celandine
Ranunculus repens	Creeping Buttercup
Reynoutria japonica	Japanese Knotweed
Rosa canina	Dog Rose
Rubus fruticosus	Bramble, Blackberry
Rubus idaeus	Raspberry
Rumex obtusifolius	Broad – leaved Dock
Sanguisorba officinalis	Great Burnet
Senecio jacobaea	Ragwort
Senecio vulgaris	Groundsel
Silene dioica	Red Campion
Silene vulgaris	Bladder Campion
Sisymbrium officinale	Hedge Mustard
Solanum dulcamara	Woody Nightshade, Bittersweet
Sonchus oleraceus	Smooth Sow-thistle
Stellaria media	Common Chickweed
Symphytum officinale	Common Comfrey
Tanacetum parthenium	Feverfew
Taraxacum officinale	Dandelion
Trifolium campestre	Hop Trefoil
Trifolium pratense	Red Clover
Trifolium repens	White Clover
Urtica dioica Stinging	Nettle
Veronica chamaedrys	Germander Speedwell, Birdseye Speedwell
Veronica hederifolia	Ivy Leaved Speedwell
Vicia cracca	Tufted Vetch

MONOCOTS

Allium ursinum	Wild Garlic
Agrostis capillaris	Common Bent
Agrostis stolonifera	Creeping Bent, Fiorin
Alopecurus pratensis	Meadow Foxtail
Dactylis glomerata	Cocksfoot
Festuca rubra	Red Fescue
Galanthus nivalis	Snowdrop
Holcus lanatus	Yorkshire Fog
Hyacinthoides non scriptum	Bluebell
Iris preudacorus	Yellow Flag
Muscari armeniacum	Grape Hyacinth
Muscari atlanticum	Spanish Bluebell
Narcissus cultivars	Garden Daffodils
Poa annua	Annual Meadow Grass
Poa trivialis	Rough Meadow Grass
Typha latifolia	Great Reed Mace

Bowling Clubs

NORTHUMBERLAND BOWLING CLUB

Named after the Duke of Northumberland and formed 1888/9. Shields Daily News of 10th April 1900 on 11th annual meeting: It was reported that the past season had been fairly dry but bitterly cold. There were currently 58 members. Mr Jas Knot offered a cup for competitions among club members of the Borough and Northumberland. Thanks were expressed to Mr Geo Taylor for the good condition that the greens had been kept. The Mayor Coun. J Eskdale was elected President for the coming year.

Shields Daily News 12th May 1902: On Saturday afternoon members of Northumberland Park Bowling Club assembled on the Green to witness the official opening of their new clubhouse. It is a handsome timber erection with a veranda on the front situated on the site of the old one. Mr Wm Chater Chairman of the Committee presided over the opening proceedings. It cost £70 was built by J G Weir Contractor of Howden and with one exception all subscriptions had come from members of the club.

Shields Daily News 11th October 1910: The 21st Annual Meeting was held last night in the Town Hall Buildings, North Shields. Mr W Chater resided who reported expenditure in the year had been £15 6s 1d and the balance in hand was £4 3s 6d. Mr Chater said it had always been customary to propose the Mayor of Borough as President for the following year but Mr J M Sutton was strongly against this and said the Club should not go beyond its own members to select a president. He said it was not known who the Mayor was going to be and he might not take the slightest interest in bowls. The President should be given to one who they knew would be interested in the welfare of the club and the custom of selecting the Mayor should be broken at once. It was agreed that the President should be elected annually from members of the club. Mr Chater was duly elected President for the ensuing year.

Council Minutes 2nd May 1972 Granted permission to install electricity in clubhouse at their own expense.

Due to falling membership Northumberland Club merged with Linskill Club on 3rd March 2007.

Northumberland Bowling Club members, 1911.

Bowling must keep you young – here's Wilf Coates aged 97 putting the first bowl down the green to open the Bowling Season on the 19th April 2009.

LINSKILL BOWLING CLUB

Named after Captain William Linskill* and formed 29th November 1904. It was reported in the Shields Daily News on 30th November 1904 that: "Last night a meeting was held in the Town Hall Buildings, North Shields with Mr John Frater presiding when a new Bowling Club was formed, taking the name of Linskill Bowling Club. It was decided to become affiliated with The Tynemouth Bowling Association and enter both the Knott and Daglish Cup Competitions next season. Mr F Leverton Harris MP consented to become the first president.

Council minutes 19th July 1905 state that Linskill Bowling Club given permission by Town Improvement Committee to erect clubhouse.

Green made square week commencing 22nd March 2004. New seats and flower tubs placed around green.

* 1st November 1849 – Tynemouth was granted a Charter of Incorporation and became a Municipal Borough with Captain William Linskill of the Dragoon Guards the first Mayor and later in 1889 the first honorary freeman of the borough. He was born in 1807 and resided at Tynemouth Lodge which was built in 1790 by his grandfather. In 1857 he moved to Warkworth and the Tynemouth Lodge Estate was sold for building land.

Tynemouth Lodge.

PERCY BOWLING CLUB

Named after Earl Percy. The Shields Daily News reported on 1st May 1893 of a newly formed institution The Percy Bowling Club, opened by Coun T.T. Bolton who as vice-president remarked there was room for a second club in the Borough. Mr F.O. Towle was chairman of the committee and Mr James Catherall was Honoury Secretary.

Shields Daily News 25th June 1895: Opening ceremony of New clubhouse built by T. Chater

Shields Daily News 8th March 1900: Annual Social.

Shields Daily News 27 February 1902: Annual Ball held at Albion Assembly Rooms.

Shields Daily News 14th October 1904: 12th Annual Meeting.

Shields Daily News 10th December 1908: 2nd Annual Whist Drive and Dance.

The first President was Lord Warkworth who donated a silver challenge cup "The Warkworth Challenge Cup" in 1894. He was Henry Percy, who predeceased his father in 1909 the Earl Percy, who became the seventh Duke of Northumberland in 1899 and died in 1918. The winner of the first competition in 1894 out of an entry of 56 was Mr J Pelton who was presented with a set of Silver mounted bowls and a prize of One Guinea.

In 1919 Ald Bolton donated "The Victory Cup" in honour of the war victory and the final was played on 27th August 1919 and won by Mr R Stenhouse Jnr.

In 1924 Mr Joe Appleby a local fish merchant and Vice President of the Club donated the "Appleby Cup" the first winner on the 27th August 1924 was Mr J Twaddle.

In 1980 Mr George Bilclough donated "The George Bilclough Pairs Cup" and was won for the first time by Mr George Johnson and Mr Ted Aspery on the 27th September 1980.

The family of the late Herbie Brown a Vice President of the club presented "The Herbie Brown Memorial Cup" in 1986 played for by members who had not won an individual trophy within the club. The first winner was Mr Sam Ord on 26th September 1986.

Linskill Bowling Clubhouse and public shelter in 1965.

Percy Bowling Club members in August 2009.

Entries from Council Minutes

1780's: Reported in the Tyne Pilot in 1839 "Spital Dene was a pleasant copsed area."

1790's: Reported in the Tyne Pilot in 1839 "Spital Dene had been grubbed up into lucrative gardens then left to decay".

1839: Tyne Pilot makes positive comments on proposals for a Park.

1872: Alderman John Foster Spence proposes a Park for the inhabitants of Shields and reports of public wanting a "Peoples Park." 7/11/1872

1877: Complaints of fights by drunks around Spital Dene Fields. 23/5/1877

1878: Land offered by Duke of Northumberland – 10 acres for use as a Park. Refused by local authority.

1878: Town Council meets to consider proposed offer of land. 15/11/1878.

1884: Work starts on Park 1st December.

1885: Skeletons found – possible site of Spital Burial Ground. Ground consecrated. 8/1/1885

07/06/1895: Letters in press re charges for admission to Park. Public meeting in opposition.

1895: Percy and Northumberland Bowling Clubs demand free entry. Councillor forced to admit he "got law wrong". 13/6/1895

20/04/10: Application made to Thames Conservancy for a Cob bird (Male Swan).

15/11/10: Councillor Maud Burnett's nephew offered a Silver Pheasant for Park. Accepted.

15/05/1912: As an experiment it was agreed to allow

Carriages to be driven through the Park at a walking pace during the months of June, July and August.

10/05/15: Mr Joseph Coates of 6 Park Avenue, wrote complaining of children running backwards and forwards on the lower Bowling Green on Sunday afternoons and evenings. Action taken – Gate on Park Avenue locked between 2 and 5pm.

16/06/15: Borough Surveyor suggested Lamplighters could be employed as Park Labourers and Park Attendants.

25/10/16: It was agreed 3 women were to be engaged to assist the Gardeners and the Borough Surveyor was to decide as to the amount of wages given.

29/05/18: Poor Childrens Holiday Association instead of taking the children into the country, took them instead to the Park and requested permission to use the Bandstand.

24/09/19: The Borough Surveyor reported that recently the Park was largely used as a playground for children doing a great deal of damage. Provision made to appoint a Park Keeper whose duties are to patrol the Park and restrain mischievous children.

25/02/20: Two guns and carriages captured by the 11th Northumberland Hussars on the Italian Front were accepted by the Council to be placed one on either side of the steps to the south of the Aviary.

25/07/22: King Edward Road widened.

27/02/24: Staff was to be increased by 1 man bringing the summer staff to 8 men and 1 boy. It was noted in 1914 there were 10 men and 1 boy.

26/09/28: It was agreed to dispose for scrap of the two German Field Guns.

25/07/28: The Tynemouth Society of Antiquaries asked the Council to take steps to preserve The Sepulchre Slab by enclosing it with a railing. Railing provided at a cost of £5.

24/04/29: A Shelter is being built on the west side of the main walk overlooking the lake.

29/07/31: Gift of a male Swan from Gateshead Council.

24/11/32: Park and Sands Committee reported the Gardener's Cottage was damp due to its foundations and the condition of the roof.

26/01/38: Committee inspected site of dismantled Bandstand and considered future layout. They also inspected the new bridge erected on the site of the wooden bridge across the Burn at the south entrance.

30/06/43: Mr H F Davies, Dairyman of Grey Street, given permission to graze ponies on land abutting Park Terrace at a rent of 1/- (one shilling i.e. 5 new pence) per month.

December 1945: Southern Dene next to the Laundry to be filled in.

September 1947: Borough Surveyor to obtain a mate for the Swan.

29/05/54: Funeral in Pet's Cemetery of Bambi a Deer Fawn.

25/01/56: Cost of draining north Lake £540 and £300 to clean southern Lake.

1957: Provision of part time female Attendants for School Holidays.

1957: Vandalism recorded – 400 Geraniums uprooted.

November 1957: A "Safety Cage" was erected on the top of the "Banana Slide".

1958: Proposed terracing of Top Field with paths and seating – never done.

January 1958: A Turnstile was erected at the Park Terrace end of the footpath on the southwest boundary of the Park.

March 1958: Morpeth Council provided Ducks for Lake.

05/06/59: Swan died.

September 1959: Provision of new entrance near St Aidan's Children's Home known as Dunn's Gate.

July 1960: North Pond filled in.

30/06/61: The "Ocean Wave" on the Playing Field to be dismantled.

September 1961: New entrance in north east corner completed.

September 1961: Steps down to Playing Field near Laundry built next to Police Box.

December 1962: Internment in Pet's Cemetery 10/6p since 1948 increased to 12/6 (62 new pence).

17/05/63: Chinese Geese attacked with a bottle on their nest on the Island and eggs stolen. Mike Coates and Mike Hodgson called Police. Later at request of Mr Bird at Gaumont Cinema Children's Saturday Club a Bird Protection Exhibition was mounted.

November 1964: Proposal for new Workmen's Cabin, toilet and tool store.

12/01/68: Three skulls found buried.

November 1968: Proposed cleaning of Pond and re-siting Island.

12/08/85: Centenary celebrations. Journal reported members of Whitley Bay Operatic Society dressed in Victorian costumes strolled around Park. There were Quoits competitions and a Bowling Tournament with participants in Victorian dress.

1990: Future of Park Keeper's House in balance, must remain boarded up until someone employed. Evening Chronicle reported 12/11/90 – still boarded up.

16/09/03: Mayor Linda Arkley announced introduction of Park Wardens to maintain a clean and safe environment in Parks.

Northumberland Park
in present times

Since the park's creation the trees have matured but unfortunately most of the largest trees in the park, the elms have succumbed to Dutch Elm Disease and will have to be felled at a time when due to their decay there are more woodpeckers resident than ever before and have successfully nested in these dead trees.

In 1937 the old wooden bridge spanning the burn near the southern entrance was replaced by a stone bridge with stones obtained from the recently demolished St Peter's Church. This had been situated at the corner of Borough Road and Clive Street and was replaced by the new St Peter's Church of England in the Balkwell Estate at a time when there was a relocation of population in the town. On the 26th January 1938 the Parks and Sands Committee inspected this new bridge. In 1945 the southern dene from the bridge to the laundry was culverted and filled in and the present playing field created. It is still possible to see under the bridge how the old arch was bricked up at this time. In 1960 the northern lake was also filled in.

Northern Lake.

Burn going into the culvert underneath the Playing Field.

It is still possible to see under the bridge how the old arch was bricked up.

Pond in late 1950's.

After Tynemouth Borough was abolished in 1974 and the gardeners who numbered around a dozen in the 1960's were later made redundant the potting sheds, keeper's cottage and cabin were demolished according to official sources "to reduce vandalism". The greenhouse which had survived the war years with its glass painted black in case reflecting light attracted the attention of enemy bombers and for its last years was used as a "Cacti House" was demolished in September 1988. In reality after North Tyneside Council scrapped its Parks Department there was no dedicated staff to maintain the standards and a period of steady decline followed. This resulted in overgrown paths, the flower beds which had lined both sides of the main walkway from the north to south gates disappearing, both public shelters overlooking the lake and bowling greens being demolished and even almost every park bench being destroyed reducing their numbers from over fifty to less than fifteen.

The landscape has changed in so much as the gardeners kept the bushes pruned which produced denser cover for nesting and roosting birds compared to the tall and spindly principally Laurels which reached in excess of 20 feet. The banks to the south of the bowling greens which are now covered in brambles were scythed, this grassland being a perfect habitat for mice and voles and much appreciated by kestrels which we no longer see hovering over these banks.

It cannot be emphasized too much what a detrimental effect the park has suffered since there was no longer a permanent

Playing field in 1950's. Showing swings, baby swings and ocean wave or as sometimes called the witch's hat.

workforce of gardeners employed there. By virtue of the fact they spent their working lives in the park they provided a continuity of care and maintenance and had a genuine sympathetic interest in the wildlife and a pride in "their park".

Annual Park Inspections were carried out and there was rivalry between the parks in the Tynemouth Borough for the best kept park and any damage done was immediately rectified. They knew every bush and tree, some gardeners could even advise the Latin names, different species of bush were pruned at different times of the year to ensure best flowering and any diseased or old stock would be replaced. During working hours and particularly relevant to school holiday times there was always a presence of workers in the park who policed and protected the flora and fauna.

From the earliest photographs there seemed always to have been Mute Swans on the lake, the last pair, named Peter and Mary, I recall raising cygnets most years. The gardeners fed them every morning with corn supplemented by bread brought by countless local children and were nicknamed the King and Queen of the park.

In the late 1950's the following poem was printed in the Shields Weekly Newspaper written by Les Silver of North

Shields dedicated to the male Mute Swan resident on the lake till its death in 1959.

Portrait of Peter

"Peter, Peter, Peter," came the voice on the autumn air,
"Peter, Peter, Peter, howway lad, wot yer deein' ower there ?
Cum an get yor breakfast, hurry up fer gudness sake,"
So Peter lifted up his head and sailed across the lake.
He moved himself with regal grace, King of Northumberland Park,
Eyes like the Ancient Mariner proud as the Cutty Sark,
He bent his head disdainfully and snorted out his food,
But ate it up obligingly when he found that it was good.

The autumn breezes rippled the lake, rustled through the grass,
Peter looked proudly at himself in his private looking glass.
While the little ducks waggled their little tails, pleased as anything,
To think that all this place was theirs, and such a handsome King.

View from Dunn's Gate (North West corner) – showing old Spital Dene Cottage in 1964 and a young Richard Coates

James "Jimmy" Chirnside who was employed by the Council for 43 years, was the last Park Keeper and resided with his family in the park house on King Edward Road until 1989. Like his Grandfather and Father before him he was a dedicated gardener and took great pride in the park, particularly the magnificent coat of arms flower beds above the pond which he personally maintained.

This picture below shows the Tynemouth County Borough Coat of Arms flower bed showing the Mayor's name Coun John Smith 1961 and 1962.

The shield at the centre of the coat of arms was that of the Prior of Tynemouth – the three crowns for the three kings, Oswin, Osred and Malcolm buried at the Priory.

The motto meaning "Our harvest is from the deeps" relates to the Miner and Fisherman on whom the growth of North Shields depended, one mining coal from deep underground and one getting fish from the depths of the sea. Tynemouth County Borough created in 1849 was replaced in April 1974 by North Tyneside MBC.

In August 1985 to celebrate the park's centenary a series of events were arranged by North Tyneside Recreation and Amenities Department commencing on Wednesday 8th with members of Whitley bay Operatic Society strolling round the park in period costume while children danced round a maypole. The next day a Punch and Judy man was in the park and gardeners were dressed in Victorian

144

costumes whilst doing their work. A full programme of events was organised for Sunday the 11th the actual 100th birthday – there were strollers in Victorian dress, a parade of motor cars that had featured in films and television and Victorian cycles. At 2pm three commemorative trees were planted by the Deputy Mayor Councillor F. Mavin, Leader of the Labour Group Councillor B. Flood and the Chairman of the Recreation and Amenities Committee Councillor W. Rickleton. This was followed by a Victorian Music Hall, a Punch and Judy Show, music by Swan Hunter's Band and a quoits competition using horseshoes.

By the early 1990's with the park keeper's house vacant and boarded up, the halcyon days of the park had gone, when the public could be proud of their Park and parents could confidently allow their children to play safely knowing there was adequate supervision, when the bowling greens and playing field had attendants, the gardeners were present and the park keeper used to ring the bell in the tower above the main greenhouse to warn of the imminent locking of the gates for the night as dusk fell. Consequently the general public, especially the older members who used to spend time in the park being deterred by the depressing spectacle and intimidated by unchecked youth almost totally abandoned the park.

Hope surfaced in 1999 in the formation of a "Friends of Northumberland Park" group by local residents who were dismayed by the neglected state of this valuable amenity. A committee was elected, a formal constitution was accepted, mission statement and objectives were agreed, regular meeting were held with North Tyneside Council in the Linskill Centre and monthly coffee mornings were held in St Augustin's Church. Weekly Saturday work parties met in the park and events to raise awareness such as an exhibition in North Shields Library and Bar-B-Qs were organised. After only three years in existence, their actions having prompted North Tyneside Council to channel more resources into maintenance of the Park coupled with a few of the main committee members not being able to commit as much time as previously to this cause it was agreed to wind up the group in the knowledge that they had made an impression.

After 12 years of no supervision or regular maintenance in 2003 Mayor Linda Arkley who had previously attended the Friends meetings introduced Park Wardens which meant that for the first time in over ten years there were permanent council employees in the park. It may never again be as in the splendour of Victorian days with immaculate flower beds, ornamental planted urns, the Tynemouth Coat of Arms above the pond created with different coloured mosses and flowers showing the current mayor's name but with the litter removed and paths kept clear, parents and children may return in numbers to feed the ducks and play on the swings and as originally intended in 1885 as an oasis in a growing conurbation for people to enjoy its natural beauty and changing seasons.

Then in 2009 with grants available from the Heritage Lottery Fund to restore and regenerate historic public parks, North Tyneside Council organised a series of exhibitions and Park Fun Days beginning on 21st March 2009 held in the park and at local venues to obtain the comments of North Tyneside residents with regard to their requirements from a public park.

In July 2009 proposals by the council were put to North Tyneside residents to extend Tynemouth Village Conservation Area to include Northumberland Park. Proposals for the park include the building of café and toilets, improving paths, restoring railings and features, provide more benches, introducing bore hole water source into the burn to enhance water flow, removing some overcrowded sycamore trees to open up original designed views and manage woodland areas.

A Regeneration Project Board was established to monitor the performance and to define its terms of reference and the inaugural meeting took place on the 22nd July. The collated information together with information regarding the historical, environmental and social importance of the park and draft proposals for its regeneration was submitted to the Heritage Lottery Fund for assessment and approval on 28th August 2009.

On the 5th July 2010 after site meetings and negotiations the Heritage Lottery Fund awarded £109,000 for development funding so that North Tyneside Council can develop the final specification for the re-generation, ahead of the £2.2 million application.

On the 11th August 2010 to celebrate the 125th anniversary of the park's official opening, North Tyneside

Council assisted by members of the public organised a party in the park which was estimated to have been attended by in excess of 1,700 visitors.

The sun shone and at 11am Mayor Linda Arkley and Councillor Glynis Barrie toured the park, escorted by members of the New Friends of the Park group and listened to Pipers Fancy, a group of eight Northumbrian Pipers who were playing in front of the Coat of Arms flower bed which was specially planted with flowers depicting the number 125.

Park Fun Day 30th August 2009.

"PIPERS FANCY".

Mike Coates, Mayor Linda Arkley, Kathleen Tutin, Councillor Glynis Barrie and Mike Tutin enjoying the 125th anniversary celebrations.

In June 2010 funded by Natural England a "link" path was created along the old Blyth and Tyne railway line to connect the park to Tynemouth Station.

The overgrown former railway line in August 2005.

The same view looking towards Tynemouth Station in January 2012.

There had always been a group of regular park users who were keen to assist in the improvement and maintenance of the park and with the increased interest generated by the Heritage Lottery Bid and with North Tyneside Councils encouragement on the 3th November 2010 "The New Friends of Northumberland Park" group was formed and formerly constituted.

This group immediately commenced submitting applications for funding from various charitable bodies to obtain materials and plants to create wildlife areas and improve flower beds within the park.

With this group now playing an active part in the park's regeneration and North Tyneside Council increased enthusiasm to protect and enhance this valuable amenity the future looks bright for this little haven which was gifted to the people of Shields over 125 years ago.

Author's postscript

As this book was about to be printed on the 1st July 2012 it was confirmed the regeneration bid had been sucessful and North Tyneside Council issued a press statement as follows: "The hundreds of park users who have rallied to rescue the historic Northumberland Park for future generations have been rewarded with a £2.2 million grant from the Heritage Lottery Fund (HLF) and the Big Lottery Fund (BIG)."

The funding will allow the reinstatement and restoration of lost features, such as the fountain and street furniture in the park, as well as creating essential new visitor facilities to support the park's long-term future.

Work will get underway in the Autumn and will be completed by late 2015.

Pow Burn in Autumn 2005.

Remains of Rustic bridge which crossed the Burn near the Pet's Cemetery.

Acknowledgements

The author wishes to express his sincere thanks to Mike Hodgson for the picture of the Fox and the pictures of birds on pages 77, 79, 85, 87 and 99; to Tom Tams for his pictures of the Nuthatch and the Purple Hairstreak butterfly; to Linda McCann for the picture of the Carr Pottery bottle; to Stew Rickard for the Garibaldi Brass Band poster and to Mike Nattrass for assistance with butterfly recording and Mike Tutin for assistance with bird recording.

To Richard Carlton and Alan Rushforth of The Archaeological Practice Ltd, Newcastle for obtaining permission for me to visit The Duke of Northumberland's Archives at Alnwick Castle for research purposes.

Images of the map on page 6 and the first lease of Spital Dean Farm on pages 22 and 23 are from the Collection of the Duke of Northumberland.

Thanks also to the staff of the Local Studies Centre at North Shields Library for their assistance.

Maps on pages 7 and 9 reproduced from 1865 and 1935 Ordnance Survey maps with the kind permission of the Ordnance Survey.

Showing the Island re-sited at the bottom of the pond, 1972.